BEGINNING CHESS

Also available from The Lyons Press

The Right Way to Play Chess

Beginning Backgammon

100 Backgammon Puzzles

BEGINNING CHESS

HOW TO MASTER THE FUNDAMENTAL SKILLS

D. B. PRITCHARD

THE LYONS PRESS

Guilford, Connecticut

An imprint of The Globe Pequot Press

Contents

Foreword

Many diagrams in this book show only a section of the chessboard to save space. Where the section includes a corner or edge of the board this is clearly illustrated, *but in every case the whole of the chessboard is in use, with the exception of the constructional problems in Part One.*

Cross-references are freely used: for example, (59*B*) refers to diagram *B* in section 59. An Index is also given at the end.

A chess set is needed to follow the latter part of the book. The standard 'Staunton pattern' men are recommended.

Introduction

Chess is very old. Its descent can be traced directly from the game of chaturanga, played in India thirteen centuries ago and probably much before that. In these early times, dice were often used to determine the man to be moved.

From India, the game spread the way things did in those days – along trade routes and in the wake of armies. In these historical movements the game underwent changes so that today we find (for example) Chinese and Japanese chess (respectively xiangqi and shogi) – both developed from the early game – played very differently from our chess.

The game moved west from India, through Persia to the Moslem lands, and into Western Europe by way of Spain and Italy in about the 9th century, but it was not until some six hundred years later that it was played in its present form.

Throughout the Middle Ages chess remained a recreation of the nobility and well-to-do, and good players, like other artists in those times, often found rich patrons to support them.

The big advances in education in the last century resulted in the game being much more widely played, and easier travel made possible contests between the best players of different countries. The first World Championship match was held in London in 1866 and since then there has been a rapid rise in the level of play. Naturally, there are and have been many great players. Mostly these have been European, but our so-called 'European chess' is now played all over the world. Teams from over a hundred nations compete in the chess 'olympics' which are held regularly.

One could make a long list of famous and clever people of the past who have been keen chessplayers but few, if any, were expert by our present standards; even Napoleon found the chessmen much more difficult to control than his armies. Skill at the game does not seem to go with any special talents, a fact from which most of us can draw encouragement.

The most important and exciting change in the history of chess has, however, taken place in our time: the game has been captured by the young. At any important gathering, including the principal international tournaments, it is youth that now holds the stage and will probably still do so thirteen hundred years hence.

This book is for the young, and even for the very young with some guidance from parent or teacher, but it is also for the adult who prefers to tread surely and does not wish to have his intellect stretched in a game. In the arrangement of the contents I have allowed myself to be guided by past pupils, for the beginner knows best the pace he can make and the method and sequence of instruction that suits him.

My aim throughout has been to keep the explanations as simple as possible, so at times I have chosen to state general truths rather than to go into detailed, if more precise descriptions. I doubt if readers will find this book at all difficult to follow, but would like to hear from any who do.

PART ONE

The Rules of Play

1
The Game

Chess is a game of skill between two players. It is played on a chessboard of 64 squares (8 × 8) coloured alternately light and dark. Each player has at his command a small army of chessmen; one is light-coloured, the other dark. The squares of the chessboard, and the chessmen, are usually white and black and are so called whatever their colour. Also, the player of the white men is called White and the player of the black men, Black.

2

At the start of a game, the chessmen are placed on the board in what is called the INITIAL POSITION. Each player moves in turn, White starting. A move is the transfer of a man from the square on which it stands to another square to which it is permitted to move. If an enemy man is standing on the square to which the move is made, then this man is captured: it is removed from the board and takes no further part in the game. Thus in a chess game the number of men on the board is reduced from time to time but never increased. No two men may occupy the same square, nor may a player capture one of his own men.

3
The Chessmen

The men on each side at the start of a game number

sixteen: One KING, one QUEEN, two ROOKS (sometimes wrongly called Castles), two BISHOPS, two KNIGHTS and eight PAWNS. They look like this in most chess sets:

| King | Queen | **Rook** | Bishop | Knight | Pawn |

| King | Queen | **Rook** | Bishop | Knight | Pawn |

They look like this in most diagrams:

| King | Queen | Rook | Bishop | Knight | Pawn |

Each man moves in a different way, but all men of the same type move in the same way. A (chess) man can mean either a PAWN or a PIECE. Notice that a pawn is not called a piece, and therefore the forces on each side at the start of a game number EIGHT PAWNS and EIGHT PIECES.

4 *Object of Game*

The object of the game is to capture the opponent's king, and the first player to do so is the winner. There are, however, a number of other ways in which a game can end, either as a win for one side or as a draw.

5 *Initial Position*

Here is the chessboard and the initial position. Each player ('White' and 'Black' in the diagrams) sits behind his own army. Observe that the board is placed so that there is a dark square in the left-hand corner in front of each player.

(Black)   (Black)

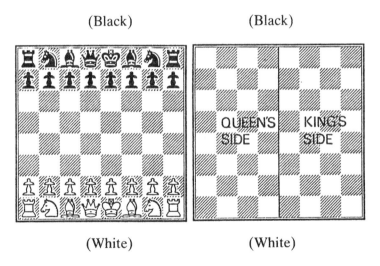

(White)   (White)

The arrangement of the pawns and pieces on the board is easy to see. Note that the queen is placed on the square of her own colour (white queen on light square, black queen on dark square) and the king on the opposite colour (white king on dark square, black king on light square). All you need remember is QUEEN ON SQUARE OF OWN

COLOUR since the king must occupy the remaining square. In all chess diagrams, WHITE is shown as playing UP the board and BLACK down the board.

6

A few chess terms are now necessary. If an imaginary line is drawn down the middle of the board from top to bottom, both queens are seen to be on one side and both kings on the other. The half of the board in which the queens stand in the initial position is called the QUEEN'S SIDE and the half in which the kings stand, the KING'S SIDE. White's king's side is therefore on his right, Black's king's side on his left. These descriptions are never changed, even when the kings and queens move around the board.

7

Files and Ranks

The lines of squares that run up and down the board are called, appropriately enough for a war game, the FILES; and those that run across the board, the RANKS.

(Black) (Black)

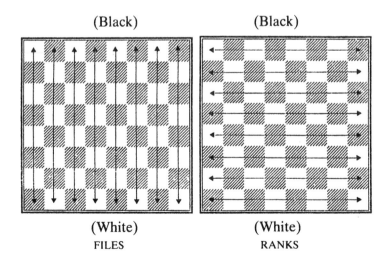

(White) (White)

FILES RANKS

12

8
Diagonals. The Centre

One also talks of DIAGONALS. There are 26 on the board, varying in length from two to eight squares as shown in the diagram. Each diagonal is made up of squares of one colour only, whereas files and ranks have squares of alternating colours.

The CENTRE is a term used to refer to the four central squares and, more loosely, the twelve squares around them. The importance of the centre in chess will become clear later.

(Black)　　　　　　(Black)

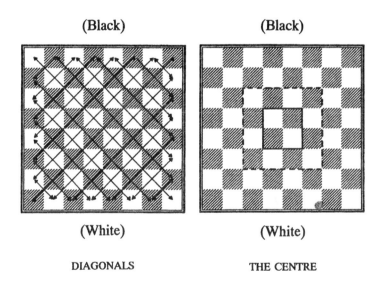

(White)　　　　　　(White)

DIAGONALS　　　　THE CENTRE

9

We now consider the separate chessmen. The moves of the king, queen, rook and bishop are easy to understand and it is only those of the knight and pawn that may prove a little difficult at first.

10
The Rook and Bishop

The ROOK moves in straight lines, vertical and horizontal (that is, along the ranks and files) and the BISHOP along the diagonals in any direction. A rook or bishop may be moved to any vacant square along any of the lines on which it stands provided that, in moving to the chosen square, there are no men of either colour in its path. If a rook or bishop may legally move to a square which is occupied by an enemy man, then that man can be captured and is at once removed from the board.

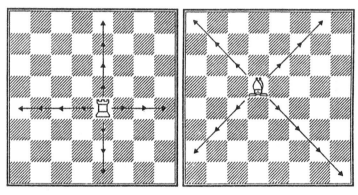

Rook's Move   Bishop's Move

It will be seen that, if unobstructed, these pieces have great freedom of action, being able to cross the board in a single move. Each move, however, may only be made in one direction. On an empty board, a rook, wherever placed, could move immediately to any one of 14 squares, and could reach any other square on the board in two moves and in each case would have two ways of doing this.

You should prove this to yourself before going further.

The bishop, because it moves on diagonals, keeps to the squares of one colour throughout the game. The bishop controls most squares if posted in the centre (13) and fewest squares (7) if on the edge of the board. Again, prove this statement to yourself.

Because the bishop can move on squares of one colour only, enemy men occupying squares of the opposite colour are safe from attack by it. Look again at the initial position and you will see that at the start of a game each player has one bishop on a white square and one on a black.

11 *Capturing*

Capturing in chess is optional. To capture an opponent's man for nothing is usually good for it means that his army is thereby reduced in strength compared with yours. This in turn will reduce his resistance thus making your task that much easier.

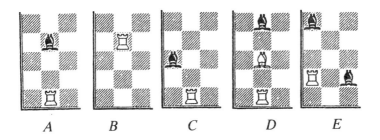

A	*B*	*C*	*D*	*E*

In many diagrams in this book only a part of the chessboard is shown to save space. The edges of the board are always shown where necessary.

In *A*, the white rook is attacking the black bishop. If it is White's turn to play, he can capture it. *B* shows the position on completion of the capture. The black bishop has been removed from the board. If it was Black's turn to move in *A*, he could escape by removing his bishop from the line of attack as, for example, in *C*. The bishop cannot attack the rook for it is on a white square. In *D*, the rook is not attacking the black bishop because there is a white bishop in the way. Were this piece to move, the rook would then be attacking the black bishop. In *E*, White, to play, could capture either bishop. If neither bishop moved (suppose Black plays somewhere else on the board), the rook could capture both of them in three moves and would have four different ways of doing this. You may care to work these out.

Do not try to memorize these or other diagrams for they are only examples. Try instead to learn the ideas. The positions in the diagrams you may never see again but the ideas they illustrate will recur many times in your games.

12

A man that is 'attacking' a square occupied by a friendly man is said to be defending or guarding it, since if his companion is captured, he will be able to retake the capturing man.

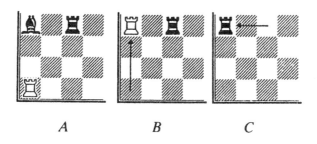

A   B   C

In *A*, the white rook is attacking the bishop which is defended by a rook. If White, on his turn to play, takes the bishop (*B*), Black can then recapture the rook (*C*). White has lost a rook and Black has lost a bishop.

13

Here are some mini-positions that will help you understand the rooks better and generally how chessmen move, attack and defend each other.

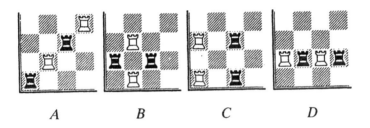

A   B   C   D

In *A*, no rook attacks or defends any other. In *B*, no rook is attacked but rooks of the same colour defend each other. In *C*, each rook defends his twin and attacks an enemy rook. Neither side can win a piece in this situation whoever is to move and regardless of what move is made (to 'win a piece' means to capture it for nothing). This may seem incredible, but try it! In *D*, each side has the option of 3 captures and whoever moves first wins a rook by making any capture. This would be true however the four rooks were arranged on the same rank or file. Again, convince yourself that this statement is correct.

14   *Exchanging*

Where a man is captured and a similar man is given up for it (a rook for a rook; a bishop for a bishop) there has been no loss to either side. This is called an EXCHANGE, and we talk of 'exchanging rooks' for example.

15

If you have anyone to play with (you can even play against yourself), you can now try your skill. Place the board with a dark square in the left-hand corner (remember!) and put the four rooks and four bishops on it so that no piece attacks an opposing piece (this is a good exercise in itself). White moves first and the winner is the player who is a piece ahead *when it is his turn to play*. This is a simple game and, like noughts and crosses, it is only possible to win if the other player makes an elementary mistake. It is a rule of chess that if you touch a man when it is your turn to play then you must move it, and if you touch one of your opponent's men, you must capture it if you can. It is good practice to play 'touch and move' at all times. Once you make a move and let go of your man, you may not change your move.

If you keep hold of the man you may play it to some other square if you wish but you must move it ('touch and move'). It is best to think out your move and then play firmly without hesitation.

16

Chess pieces in their movements form patterns. These patterns show the relationship between the different men and the limits that the chessboard places on them.

Below, and elsewhere in this Part, short problems are given in which you will be able to discover these patterns for yourself and so come to appreciate the strengths and weaknesses of the various men. This will help you to see deeper into the game and play better.

There are several possible solutions to each problem,

none of them difficult. Examples are illustrated at the end of the Part.

ALL PROBLEMS ARE ON A QUARTER-BOARD (4 × 4) ONLY.

Construct I Place the white rooks and bishops (one of these on each colour) so that no piece guards any other.

Construct II Arrange the same four men so that each piece defends, and is defended by, one other piece.

17
The Queen and King

The QUEEN'S move is a combination of those of rook and bishop. The queen can therefore move in any direction in a straight line. She is the most powerful piece on the board.

The KING moves like the queen but only one square at a time. A king thus commands eight squares if not on the edge of the board, five squares on the edge and three squares if he is standing in a corner.

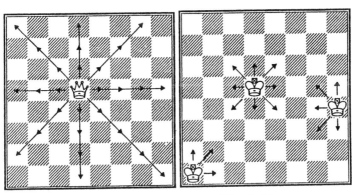

Queen's Move   King's Move

18

We have said that the object of the game is to capture the opponent's king. A king which is attacked and therefore threatened with capture on the next move is said to be in CHECK. When you attack your opponent's king say 'Check'; it is a good practice though not compulsory.

If the king is unable to escape from a check it is CHECKMATE and the game is over.

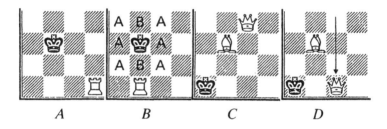

A	*B*	*C*	*D*

In *A*, the white rook moves and puts the black king in check (*B*). It is check because the rook is threatening to take off the king next move. It is not checkmate because the king has a choice of six squares (marked A) to which to move to escape capture. The king may not move to the two squares marked (B) because on either of these he would still be in check from the rook.

It is a rule that the side whose king is in check must immediately get out of check. There are three possible ways of doing this, all or any of which may be playable in a given position:

(1) The king may move to a square which is not attacked by an enemy man;
(2) The man giving check may be captured;
(3) A defender may be placed between the attacker and the king.

If none is possible, then the king is checkmate and the game is over.

In *C* the white queen moves to give check (*D*). Black cannot escape this check as the three squares to which the king could normally move are attacked either by the queen or the bishop. The position is checkmate. The black king is lost and the game is over.

While checkmate is always the best move you can make in a game, a move that gives check is not necessarily good or bad. Many beginners make the mistake of giving check whenever they can, possibly because they enjoy announcing it.

19

You will now be aware that the king is never actually captured in chess: the game is over when one side cannot avoid loss of his king on the next move. In other respects, the king may move and capture like any other piece. He cannot, of course, capture a defended man because by so doing he would be moving into check. *The two kings cannot stand next to each other because they would both then be in check.* This is an important consideration towards the end of the game as we shall see.

20

The following mini-positions will help you further to understand 'check' and 'checkmate'.

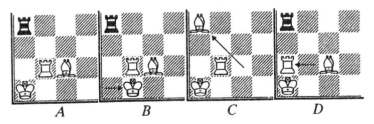

| A | B | C | D |

In *A*, the white king is in check from the black rook. White must now get out of check at once. He may move the king (*B*), capture the attacking piece with his bishop (*C*) or interpose a rook (*D*), as he pleases. Here is another situation:

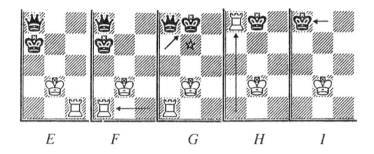

E   F   G   H   I

White moves in *E* and checks the black king (*F*). The king moves out of check (*G*) since the attacker could not be captured and no man could be interposed anyway. Note that the king had an alternative square (marked *) to which he could have moved to escape the check. In *H*, the rook has captured the queen, again giving check to the black king. In *I*, the king recaptures the rook; a legal move since the piece was not defended. The king has not been checkmated but Black has lost a queen for a rook. Lastly, a sequence of moves ending in checkmate:

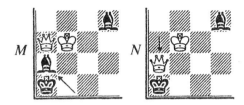

In *J*, the white queen has just given check. The only way Black can escape the check is to interpose the bishop (*K*): he cannot move his king forward as it would then stand next to the white king, which is illegal. In *L*, the queen, moving like a bishop, has again checked the black king. *M* shows the position after Black's only move: again interposing the bishop and at the same time giving check to the white king. *N* shows the end of the game. The queen, moving like a rook, has captured the black bishop simultaneously releasing the white king from check and checkmating the black king. The king cannot take the queen as the queen is defended by the white king. It may help you to play this sequence through again. Can you see the defensive role of the bishop that does not move? White has forced a MATE (checkmate is usually simply called 'mate') in three moves.

21

Here are a few more problems to help you become familiar with the pieces we have studied. Again, all are on the quarter-board.

Construct III   Place four white queens so that none is defended (you can use pawns to represent queens).

23

Construct IV   Construct checkmate positions using both kings and, in turn, the following white men: (1) Queen and rook; (2) Queen; (3) Two rooks; (4) Rook and bishop; (5) Rook; (6) Two bishops.

Construct V   Arrange a king, queen, rook and bishop of each colour so that no man of either side is attacked.

22
The Knight

We shall return to checkmate later, but let us now look at the KNIGHT. The knight is the most attractive of chess pieces, both in appearance and on account of its move. The knight's move may be described in different ways:

(1) As the letter 'L';
(2) The next square but one of a different colour;
(3) One square horizontally or vertically, then one square diagonally in the same direction;
(4) The opposite corner of a 3 × 2 rectangle.

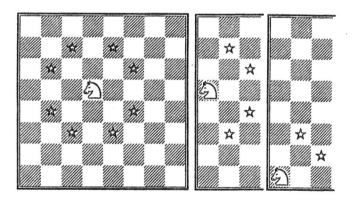

Knight's Move

24

The Rules of Play

In these three positions, the knight's move is to any of the starred squares. The knight moves directly to the chosen square: it does not follow a path like the queen, rook or bishop. This is an important feature of the knight for it means that its movement cannot be blocked by other men. It will be seen from the diagrams that the knight's power is reduced near or at the edge of the board and is further reduced next to or in a corner. The knight always attacks squares of the opposite colour to the square on which it stands. Each move therefore the knight 'changes colour'. The knight captures in a similar way to the other pieces.

The knight's freedom of movement is well shown in *A*. Despite being surrounded by black men, it can escape to any of eight squares, although only on one of these squares will it not be attacked. Can you see which one?

Although free to move, a knight is weak at close quarters for it attacks none of the adjoining squares. In *B*, all the white pieces are attacking the knight. Furthermore, it cannot escape as all six squares to which it may move are controlled by the white queen.

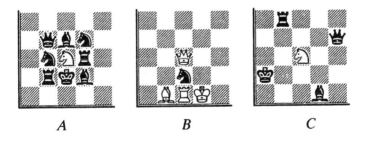

| A | B | C |

In *C*, the knight attacks all the black men simultaneously. The king, which is in check, will have to move when the knight will be free to capture one of the black pieces. This example shows the knight at its best.

23

Before you try some more problems, look again at CONSTRUCT III. If you solved this, you will now see that the four queens were separated from each other by knight moves.

Construct VI	Put any four of the five white pieces (king, queen, rook, bishop and knight) on a quarter-board so that no man guards any other. Try each combination of pieces in turn.
Construct VII	Place a white king, bishop and knight so that the knight has no move.
Construct VIII	Set up a checkmate position using a king and a knight of each colour.
Construct IX	Place the eight black pieces on a quarter-board together with the white king so that White is not in check and has a choice of three captures.
Construct X	Arrange the two kings together with a white queen, rook, bishop and knight so that each of the four white pieces can mate in one move.

24
The Pawn

This brings us to the PAWN, a man often scorned by beginners but treasured by the experts.

The pawn moves FORWARD only, ONE square at a time along the file on which it stands. Each pawn may, however, advance TWO squares on its first move. This double jump is optional.

Unlike the pieces, the pawn captures in a different way to which it moves. The pawn attacks the two squares diagonally forward, one on either side, unless the pawn stands on the edge of the board when it attacks only one square. The capture is carried out in the same manner as with the pieces: the pawn moves on to the square occupied by the enemy man, which is removed from the board.

In *A*, the white pawn can move one or two squares as its position indicates that it has not moved from the start of the game (as a pawn moves only forward, it is not possible for it to have moved and then returned to its original

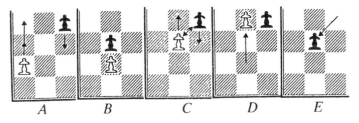

Pawn's Move

square). The black pawn in *A* can move only one square forward as it has clearly already moved. In *B*, neither pawn can move. A pawn, like all other men, can only move onto an occupied square to capture – and pawns do not capture vertically forward. In *C*, either pawn may move one square forward or capture the opposing pawn, depending on whose move it is.

A special situation is illustrated in *D*. The white pawn has just made the initial double move. *The black pawn may now capture it as though it had only moved one square.* *E* shows the position after the capture, with the white pawn removed from the board. This special move is called EN PASSANT (French for 'in passing') and can only take place between two pawns. The capture must be made at once (that is, on the next move) or this right is lost. An

27

'en passant' capture is optional. As this move is the one that gives most trouble to beginners, repetition may help:

(1) The 'en passant' move can only take place after the initial two-square move of a pawn;

(2) The capture can be made only by an opposing pawn that could legally have captured the adversary if it had moved one square;

(3) The capture is made by placing the capturing pawn on the square over which his victim has passed, removing the captured pawn from the board. You will see that this move is similar to an orthodox pawn capture: one square diagonally forward. This is the only case in chess where a man making a capture moves to a square other than that occupied by the man being captured;

(4) The right to take 'en passant' must be exercised at once or the privilege is lost.

25

Here we look at some more pawn situations.

In *A*, the white pawn has four possible moves: it can move one or two squares forward or it can capture either of the black men. In *B*, no pawns can move. The middle pawn could only have got where it is by making a capture from its initial square. The white pawns are said to be DOUBLED. It is not uncommon to have three pawns of the same colour on one file.

All four pawns in *C* can only move to capture, and each has one available capture. Black is threatening to take off the white pawn in *D*. White can evade the threat by advancing the free pawn one square, when all four pawns will be without a move (*E*) or by capturing the black

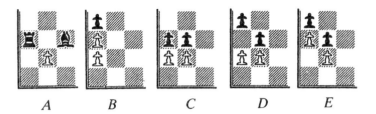

A   B   C   D   E

pawn. If the white pawn takes the black pawn, the second black pawn could recapture when there would be only two pawns left – one of each colour – neither of which will be able to move. We are back to position *B* in the previous section.

26 *Pawn Promotion*

You may be wondering what happens to a pawn when it arrives at the end of the board (if you have read *Alice Through the Looking Glass* you will already know!). A pawn on reaching the last rank is promoted to any piece, *other than a king,* at the player's choice. Promotion is compulsory – it cannot remain a pawn. The promotion move is made by placing the piece chosen on the promotion square and removing the pawn from the board. If the pawn on promotion simultaneously captures an enemy piece, then of course this piece is also taken off the board.

Since the queen is the most powerful piece, a pawn is almost invariably promoted to queen (the promotion square is often called the QUEENING SQUARE). The move is completed by promotion, and thereafter the promoted piece behaves in the same manner as a queen (or whatever piece is chosen).

The pieces remaining on the board at the time of promotion do not affect the choice of piece. It is not unusual in a game for one side to have two queens on the board; nine are possible but unheard of! (If you don't have a second queen to hand, substitute an inverted rook or a token.)

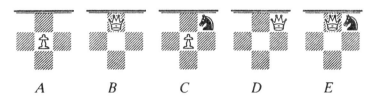

A   B   C   D   E

A–B shows the promotion of a pawn to queen; *A* before the move and *B* on completion of the move. *C–D* is the same sequence but this time the pawn promotes in making a capture. Notice that the pawn could also have been promoted by moving straight forward one square (*E*).

Now you will see why pawns are not to be scorned: each one is a potential queen. A pawn's journey to promotion is a long one and is unlikely to be achieved until most of the pieces are gone from the board. The side that 'queens a pawn' first is often in a position to win quickly.

27

Back now to a few problems on the quarter board.

Construct XI	Place eight pawns (four of each colour) so that none may move or capture.
Construct XII	Place the same eight pawns so that each side has six different captures.
Construct XIII	Arrange the two kings and one white pawn so that white can promote and give checkmate in one move.
Construct XIV	Set up a checkmate position, without promotion, using only king and one pawn of each colour.

30

Construct XV Construct a position in which a pawn can play to any one of four squares and is at no time attacked.

Construct XVI Construct a position in which one pawn may make any one of twelve different moves and is at no time itself attacked (if you solved XV you have practically solved this!).

28
Values of the Men

You may already have formed an opinion about the worth of some of the chessmen. Here is a table of relative values:

Pawn–1 Knight–3 Bishop–3 Rook–5 Queen–9

No value is given to the king since he cannot be exchanged. His powers are about equal to those of a knight or bishop.

The values given are only approximate (in fact, two bishops are much better than rook and pawn although both count six points) but you should be guided by them when making captures and exchanges. For example, if you give up your queen for rook, bishop and three pawns, you will see that this is to your advantage (nine points against eleven). Later you will see how the values of the men vary even from move to move, according to the position.

29

A few more common terms may be useful here:

The queen and rooks are known as the MAJOR PIECES.

The bishops and knights are known as MINOR PIECES.

To gain a rook for the loss of a knight or bishop is to WIN THE EXCHANGE.

30
Castling

There is a special move in chess that both players may

make once in every game. This special move is called CASTLING. Two men – the king and one rook – which must be on their original squares, move together, the single exception to the rule that only one man may move at a time.

Castling consists of moving the king two squares towards the rook and then bringing the rook to the square next to the king on the inside. It is a rule that the king shall be moved first when castling.

When this double move takes place on the king's side, it is called king's side castling, and on the queen's side, queen's side castling.

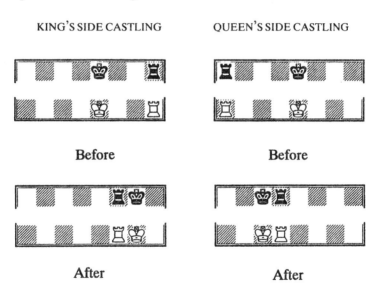

KING'S SIDE CASTLING   QUEEN'S SIDE CASTLING

Before   Before

After   After

A player may castle at any time provided that certain conditions are met:

(1) The king and the chosen rook have not been moved.

32

(2) There is no man of either colour between the king and the rook.

(3) The king is not in check at the time, nor will he in castling pass through check, nor will he be in check when castling is completed.

A, B, C and *D* illustrate four cases where castling is not possible. *A* – the rook has moved; *B* – the king is in check; *C* – the king would pass through check; *D* – the king would be in check on completion of castling.

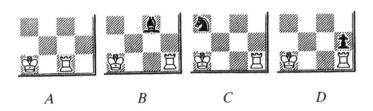

| A | B | C | D |

Castling achieves two things:
(1) It removes the king from the middle of the board where it is in most danger.
(2) It brings a rook from the corner into the centre where the piece is more active.

Castling is optional, and there is no such move as 'un-castling'. The right to castle should not be given up easily as it is a very useful move. Castling is used by both players in most games.

It is a common belief that once a king has been checked it may not castle. This is not so, as the above rules should make clear.

31   *Stalemate and Zugzwang*

To close our review of the main rules of the game, mention must be made of a situation which is sometimes reached where a side whose turn it is to play has no legal move. This situation is known as STALEMATE and is only likely to occur when there are few men left on the board. Stalemate is a draw, and the game is over.

A player cannot choose not to move just because it would lead to certain loss. If there is a legal move on the board it must be made. This situation, which does not end the game, is known as ZUGZWANG (German: 'forced move'). Stalemate is quite common among beginners (particularly where one side has only a king left),

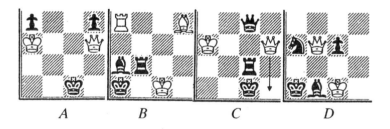

A   B   C   D

zugzwang more common between experienced players.

A typical stalemate position is shown at *A*. Black, to move, is unable to do so. In *B*, Black, to move, is again stalemated as neither the rook nor the bishop can move without exposing the king to check, whilst the king may not move next to the white king. With White to play, however, the game is checkmate as White can take the rook off with the bishop which is then defended by the king. The black king is in check and has no escape. White is a rook behind in *C* and his king is in peril – normally a hopeless position. However, he can here save the game by an ingenious sacrifice, as shown. The black king must take the queen as it is the only legal move – and White is then stalemated! *D* is an amusing example of zugzwang. Black, who is not threatened with an immediate checkmate, is

34

forced to move. Whichever man he moves he is check-mated next play. The mates are worth working out as they demonstrate the great power of the queen.

32

Finally, a few more quarter-board exercises.

Construct XVII Place a black king, bishop & pawn and a white king & bishop so that Black is stalemated.

Construct XVIII Set up a stalemate position using a white king & pawn and the two black rooks and putting no man on the edge of the board.

Construct XIX Arrange any men so that White can play pawn takes pawn 'en passant', at the same time giving checkmate.

Construct XX Arrange any men so that White can play Castles, at the same time giving check-mate.

33 *Examples of Construction Problems*
Below are example answers to construction problems given in this Part. Other solutions to those shown are possible in most cases. Remember that these problems were designed to exercise your understanding of the various pieces and their behaviour – they do NOT represent positions you are ever likely to see in games. The Roman numeral below each diagram corresponds to the problem number in the text. If you found these difficult, it will be helpful to compare each problem with the given solution.

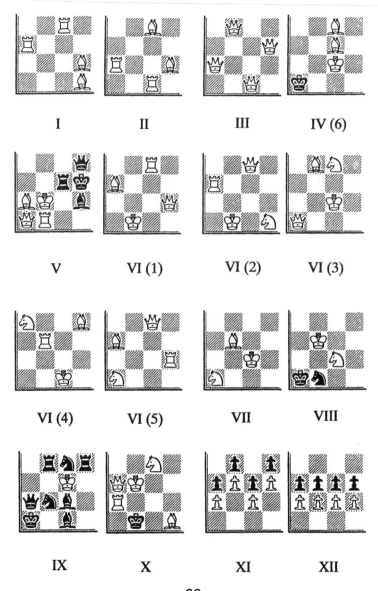

I	II

III   IV (6)

V   VI (1)   VI (2)   VI (3)

VI (4)   VI (5)   VII   VIII

IX   X   XI   XII

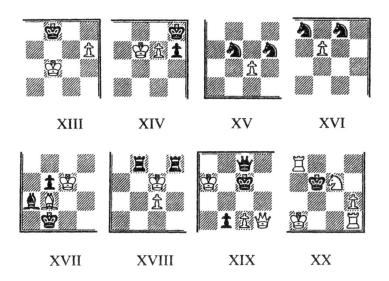

XIII XIV XV XVI

XVII XVIII XIX XX

PART TWO

Tactics

34

All the important rules of the game have now been explained and we are ready to examine tactics – the battles large and small between the two armies in close contact with each other.

The main aims of play we have already discussed. Foremost, to checkmate the opponent's king for this is the object of the game. Secondly, to try to *win material* – to capture men for nothing or to capture men of greater value than you lose. The purpose in winning material is to make it easier to force mate. The more material you win, clearly the easier it will be to do this.

35   *Combinations*

We have seen briefly how the different men work together and in opposition. It is now time to look at ways of winning material and of forcing checkmate. Certain simple manoeuvres, or *combinations* as they are called in chess, occur frequently. In fact, even the most complex play can be reduced to one or other of several basic combinations. These combinations are quite easy to understand in their bare outlines but the situations in which they arise are usually confused by the presence of other men that have no part in the particular manoeuvre. Combinations then, although familiar, have to be looked for, like objects hidden in a puzzle picture. However, it is not enough to wait idly for combinations to turn up; you will try to direct your play to make favourable combinations possible. The basic positions given in the rest of this Part will be repeated again and again in your games although not necessarily in the exact forms you see them here. You will soon know them all well.

36 *Threatened Men*

We have already met attack and defence in its simplest form in section 11.

Let us look at it again in a little more depth.

The situation in *A* is one of the most common in chess and may occur several times during the course of a game. One man attacks another man with the intention of capturing it next move. In *A* the rook has just moved to attack the bishop. We call this a THREAT as it threatens to win the bishop for nothing. The bishop is said to be EN PRISE (French: in a position to be taken).

In *B* there is no threat as the bishop is defended by a pawn (which, you will recall, captures diagonally forward). To capture the bishop would now cost White his rook, which would be a bad move as a rook is worth more than a bishop.

In *C*, the bishop has just moved to attack the rook. This is a threat because although the rook is defended, it is worth more than the bishop and White on his next play will capture it, given the opportunity.

37

There are a number of ways to meet a simple threat:
- (a) The man making the threat may be captured;
- (b) The man under attack may move away;
- (c) A friendly man may be placed between the attacker and the man attacked.

These ways of answering a threat are the same as those open to a player whose king is in check. This is not surprising as a check is no more than a simple threat to the king. However, there is no obligation here to rescue the attacked man, so that two further possibilities are open to the defender:
- (d) The attacked man may be defended if it is of equal or lesser value than the attacker;
- (e) The threat may be ignored if it appears that there is a better move elsewhere on the board. A man given up in this way is said to be *sacrificed*. Sacrifices are the sugar and spice of chess, as you will discover.

38

A man that is defended once may be attacked twice – that is, by two enemy men. This means that the defender will lose both his men in exchange for only one attacker. If the attacker is worth less than these two men together, then a threat exists.

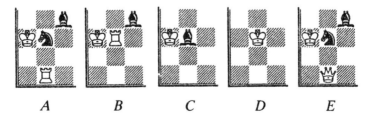

A   B   C   D   E

A–D should make this clear. In *A*, White has two men attacking the knight which is defended once. Since bishop and knight are together worth six points and a rook only five, White is threatening to capture the knight.

If Black does nothing about this, the sequence of moves *B–D* follows. In *E*, White again has two men attacking the knight, but since the queen is worth nine points against the six of bishop and knight together, Black is not threatened here.

39

Sometimes both sides build up their forces around one man, often a pawn. Although a number of men may be involved, the same principle applies: if, in a series of exchanges, the defender will lose more than the attacker, a threat exists.

In *A*, White has four men attacking the advanced pawn whilst Black has only three men defending it (notice that the second black rook is only indirectly defending the pawn: he cannot take part in the battle until his companion has engaged the enemy – this second rook acts rather like a reserve waiting in the rear).

Further, the black men are together valued at 14 points against 11 points for the white men (excluding the king,

A   *B*

which cannot of course be captured). White is therefore

41

threatening to capture the pawn. The capture would be
made by either knight or bishop. If it were made by the
white rook, the black knight would recapture and Black
would then break off the engagement. Remember that
capturing is not compulsory and neither side need make
an unfavourable capture. Now look at *B*. Again White has
four men attacking the pawn and only three black men
defending it, but here the value of the attacking force is
much greater than that of the defending force. If a white
piece now takes the pawn, White will lose material so
there is no threat to the pawn in the position given.

40

A move may threaten not just one man, but two or
sometimes more men. This is a double or multiple threat
and is much more dangerous than a simple threat because
it is harder to defend.

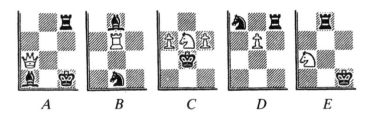

A   B   C   D   E

These are examples of double and multiple threats. In
A, the queen attacks both bishop and rook simultaneously, one of which will be captured next move. In *B*,
the rook attacks both bishop and knight. Only one can
escape. In *C*, the king has got behind the pawns and is
attacking three men at once. Only one man can move to
safety and Black will then have the choice of capturing
either of the remaining two. In *D*, a pawn attacks both a
rook and a knight.

Again, a piece is lost, only this time the attacker will die also as the rook can be moved away so as to maintain the guard on the knight. In *E*, the knight attacks both the king and the rook. The king is in check, so must move when the knight will capture the rook for nothing. These last two examples are known as FORKS since the attack resembles the prongs of a fork. A multiple fork was shown in 22*C*.

41

Possible defences against multiple threats may suggest themselves. The plan open to Black in 40*D* above, although of little help there, would have been good in 40*A* if the black king had not been present. This should be clear in *A*–*B* below: one of the attacked pieces moves away to defend the other one. Another idea would be to move one of the men attacked to make a threat elsewhere. *C*–*D* is an example. The knight has forked the two rooks but one of these is able to escape with a check, forcing the

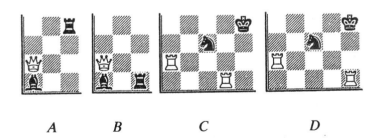

A	*B*	*C*	*D*

black king to move, when the second rook will be moved to safety – a good example of a useful check.

42   *The Pin*

Yet another idea might be to prevent the attacking man from moving. This is a common tactic known as a PIN. A pin describes a situation where a man may not move, or may not move freely, because of the action of an enemy piece.

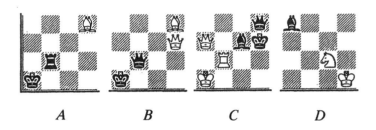

A   B   C   D

In *A*, the rook may not move at all because the king would then be in check from the bishop with White to move, which is forbidden. The rook is said to be pinned – an appropriate description. The queen in *B* can move, but only on the line of the bishop as otherwise the black king would be in check. The queen is said to be pinned even though she has some movement. In *A* and *B*, Black can free himself from the pin by moving his king. However, this will not save him for White will then capture at once in each case and Black is certain to lose material – a rook for a bishop in *A* and a queen for a bishop in *B*.

We have already had an example of pins: look back to 31*B* and you will see that the black rook and bishop are both pinned. We can now add the pin to the list of defences against a simple threat given in 37.

It is possible for a pinning piece to be itself pinned, as the black bishop in *C*. White could now free the rook by moving his king and the rook could not be captured as the bishop is pinned. If Black in turn frees himself from the pin by moving his king, White will have time to move his rook to safety.

44

D shows the most common type of pin – bishop against knight. There is no threat in this case as the knight, which is worth about the same as the bishop, is guarded. However, a pin like this cannot be said to be harmless because whereas the attacker is active, the pinned piece is, for the time being, useless – it is a 'non-piece'!

43

So far we have examined pins where it is illegal for the pinned piece to move or to move off a line. But a man that may legally move freely is also said to be pinned if it

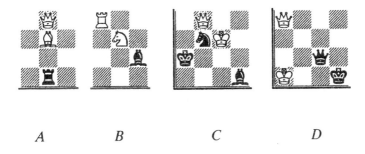

A	*B*	*C*	*D*

cannot be moved without loss of some kind.

If in *A* the bishop moves, the queen is lost. Note that in the position the rook is not threatening the bishop as that piece is guarded by the queen. The bishop is said to be pinned. Here the queen could free the pin by moving to any of the four next-door squares, keeping guard on the bishop.

The knight is pinned in *B* because if it moves the bishop will take the rook. Further, the bishop threatens the knight. Here White can free himself by moving the rook to one of the two squares where it guards the knight.

In *C* also the knight is pinned, as if it moves the white

queen will give checkmate at once. *D* illustrates a position that sometimes causes confusion. The white king cannot move even though the black queen is pinned. A pinned piece may still give check (and it is even possible for it to give checkmate if the pinning piece is itself pinned!).

44 *Discovered Attacks*

A multiple threat may take the form of a simultaneous attack by two (rarely more) pieces. In *A*, White is attacking neither of the black pieces; but after moving (*B*) both black pieces are attacked and one is lost. The power of the DISCOVERED ATTACK, as this tactic is called, can be considerable.

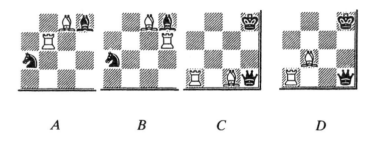

A   B   C   D

C illustrates a more dangerous form of the discovered attack: the piece that moves gives check (*D*). As Black must move his king, the queen is lost.

Below are two further types of discovered attack. Look at *E*. Here the king would be in check from the rook if the rook were not masked by the bishop. Since any move of the bishop will require that the rook check be answered, the bishop can be considered to have a 'free' move. Black

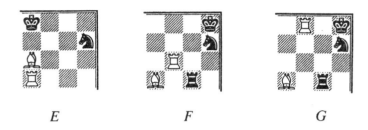

E   F   G

loses the knight to a bishop attack. This is called a DISCOVERED CHECK.

F shows an attack directed wholly against the king. Again, a masking piece moves to discover check (*G*), but this time the piece that moves also attacks the king. This is a DOUBLE CHECK. Although both the attacking pieces here are under attack themselves, neither can be captured as this would still leave the king in check from the remaining piece. Again, Black could interpose a piece between the king and either of the attackers but could not cover both attacks in the one move. In reply to a double check therefore *the King must move*. In the example the king has no move and so the position is checkmate.

45

Overleaf at *A* is this same position but without the black knight. Now White would gain nothing by the double check as the black king can move to safety (*B*). Correct for White would be *C* when the black rook would have to play as shown to escape capture. Black has been forced to pin his own rook and White could now 'win the exchange' (29) by taking off the rook with the bishop.

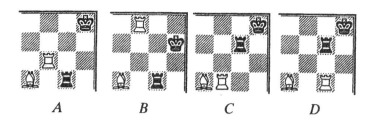

A   B   C   D

But he can do better: the rook is pinned, and White has only to attack it with his rook (as for example in *D*) to gain it for nothing next move. This example well illustrates the weakness of a pinned piece.

46   *The Skewer*

Another common tactical manoeuvre is the SKEWER. Two men, one of which may be the king, are attacked on a line.

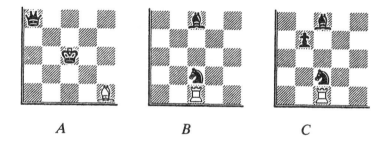

A   B   C

If the man immediately threatened moves, the second man is lost. *A* and *B* are examples. Compare *B* with 40*B*. In *C*, Black has a sufficient defence in moving up the pawn one square to guard the knight.

47

A pinned man is vulnerable to attack as we saw in 45*D*. Look at *A*, which is similar to 46*C* but with an added white pawn. Black has defended himself against the skewer by advancing the pawn to defend the knight. However, the knight is now pinned and the attack by the white pawn (*B*) wins a piece. Notice, however, that Black can choose which piece to move to safety.

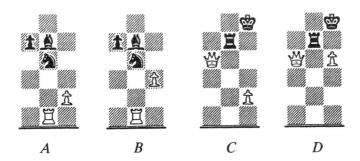

A	*B*	*C*	*D*

C–D is another example of the dangers that threaten pinned men. Here the rook may not legally move so that the pawn advance wins the piece for nothing.

48 *Overworked Men*

Our next diagrams demonstrate a common weakness: overworked men. The pawn in *A* is guarding both the rook and the bishop. White can take advantage of this in the sequence *B–D*, winning the bishop. *E* shows a variation of this: the black queen is defending against a mate and is also guarding the rook. If the rook is captured (*F*), Black cannot retake or he is mated (*G*).

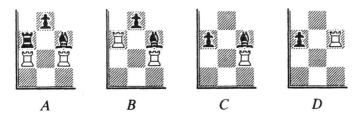

A	*B*	*C*	*D*

E   F   G

49
Piece Traps

A pinned man is without defence and is easily lost but a free man may also be trapped. Traps of this kind have one common feature: the man attacked has no square to which to escape. Different traps catch different men. Below are some of the commonest.

The queen is the hardest piece to trap because escape must be stopped in all directions. A queen that enters the enemy army alone may get into trouble: in *A*, the black queen has unwisely taken a pawn at the same time attacking the rook. Now White shuts the trap with a knight, which also defends the rook (*B*). Next move he will attack the queen with his other knight, when the queen will have no escape. In *C*, if the queen takes the unguarded pawn she is lost for a rook after Black's reply (*D*).

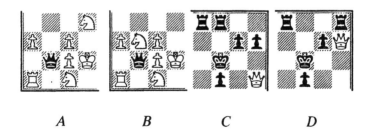

A   B   C   D

These two examples show the most frequent way in which queens are trapped: by the unwise capture of a flank pawn. The queen is rarely trapped in the middle of the board.

50

A rook too is hard to snare. The file on which the rook stands may sometimes be closed by a minor piece (*A–B*). Here a rook falls for bishop and pawn. A rook that can

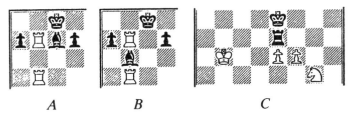

| A | B | C |

only move along a rank can sometimes be caught with surprising ease. In *C*, the rook has no safe square from the pawn attack.

51

Bishops are often trapped. Probably the commonest of all piece traps is illustrated in *A–B*. The advance of the white pawns hems in the piece. The trap is seen in many forms but almost always depends on the bishop's retreat being blocked by its own men.

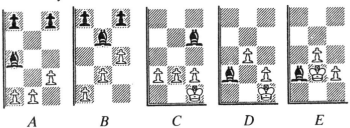

| A | B | C | D | E |

A venturesome bishop may fare no better. If the pawn is taken in *C*, White can close the line of retreat (*D*) and next move play the king (*E*) to win the bishop for two pawns.

52

A knight can be caught on the edge of the board in a situation that is common early in the game. In *A*, White has just played the pawn forward, attacking the piece. To move the knight to the side of the board now (*B*) would be

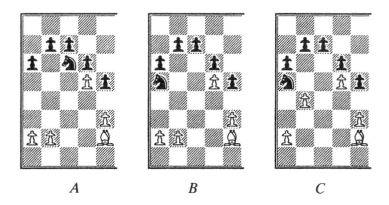

A   B   C

a bad mistake, as after another pawn move (*C*) the piece has no square for escape.

53

A pawn may also be trapped if it advances too far. Without support from a friendly pawn, it will be lost if a superior force can be brought against it (39*A*). Consider all pawn advances very carefully: remember, pawns cannot be moved back if danger threatens!

54

You will meet these traps often in your play. If you know them well they will earn you – or save you – many games. A final and important point. If you have the misfortune to have a piece trapped, do not just leave it to be taken off for nothing; capture the best enemy man you can, even if it's only a pawn. For example, in *A* take off the bishop with the rook and in *B* capture the pawn with the knight. If no capture is possible, you may be able to play your man so that your opponent must take it in a way less favourable to him. See *C*; the knight is trapped. Play as in *D* and Black must capture (*E*) or allow the piece to escape. Black's pawns are doubled and weak, as we shall see.

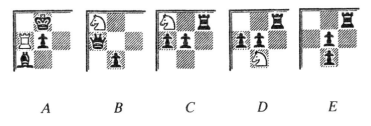

| *A* | *B* | *C* | *D* | *E* |

55
The Sacrifice

Sacrifices, we said earlier, add greatly to the pleasure of the game. One can get a lot of satisfaction out of allowing a piece to be captured in order later to force an advantage. One merit of a sacrifice is that it often comes as a surprise to the second player, and the unexpected is always a little disturbing. If your opponent puts (say) a knight 'en prise', you may suspect a trap. What is coming next? In this situation a timid player is frightened into defence, yet the move may be simply a mistake. Even intentional sacrifices are often unsound (that is, they fail against the best defence). Never be afraid to accept a sacrifice if you can see no good reason for it.

A sacrifice is not a means in itself but a means to an end. Here are two examples. In *A*, White has just played the rook on to an undefended square. Since this move is a check and also a double attack such as we saw in 40, it is forcing, Black's only sensible reply being to capture the rook, when the knight moves (*B*) forking king and queen.

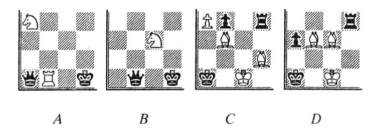

A   B   C   D

See now that the king must move next to the queen in order to recapture the knight after the queen is taken. Even so, White has gained from the combination. In *C*, White has just made the initial two-square move with his pawn. If Black accepts the sacrifice by taking the pawn 'en passant' (24), then he is mated (*D*).

56 *Examples of Checkmate*

It is now time to consider some typical checkmate positions and a little of the play that may lead up to them. In order to checkmate, we must do two things at the same time:

    (*a*) Put the king in check so that the attacking man cannot be taken and no defending man can be placed between them;

    (*b*) Ensure that all the squares around the king are

attacked, or are occupied by defenders.

Put like that, it sounds quite difficult, for if the king is away from the edge of the board there are no less than eight squares to cover in addition to the square on which he stands. However, if the king is at the edge of the board there are only five possible escape squares (or *flight squares* as they are sometimes called) and in the corner this number is reduced to three. It is therefore easier still if he is in the corner. It is usually much simpler to drive a king to the side by a series of checks rather than attempt a checkmate in the middle of the board. As it happens, though, the kings tend to spend most of their time at the edge of the board anyway!

57

Broadly speaking, the play leading to checkmate may be of two kinds:

(*a*) Direct, forceful play, where every move is urgent as the defender will, if given the chance, quickly counter-attack. This type of situation usually occurs in games where forces are about even and one side has succeeded in working up an attack on the king, perhaps at the cost of a sacrifice.

(*b*) Steady, less anxious play in which the attacker has a much stronger force and the issue is not whether he will be able to force checkmate, but when. A few small inaccuracies in the attack under these circumstances are unimportant as they are only likely to delay the checkmate, not to forfeit it.

58

First let us look at some common mating positions. You should quickly learn to recognize them on sight. Better still, you should try to see them coming so that you can either force them or defend against them.

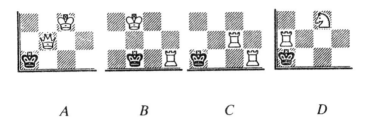

A   B   C   D

Notice how the king and queen work together against a bare king (A). Several similar mating positions are possible with these three pieces. Can you find some? B shows the mating position with a rook against a bare king. Observe how the white king guards all the squares to which his rival might move to escape check. These two examples well illustrate the rule that kings may not stand next to each other. In C a second rook is doing the same job as the king in B. D is less common but not unusual. In the last three examples, a queen could of course do the same job as a rook.

59

All the above positions would be most likely to arise under the conditions described in 57(b). The next are examples of mating positions more likely to arise from forceful play when there are still many men on the board 57(a). You will see that in each case the king is in the castled position.

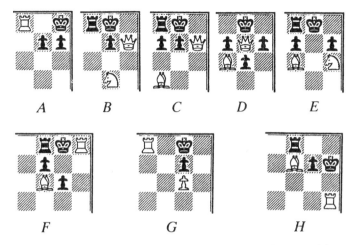

A is perhaps the commonest of all mating positions. The king is doomed because his natural flight squares are occupied by his own unmoved pawns. All the other examples are also common. *H* is a variation of *G*. Both show a well-known mating idea the elements of which are:

(*a*) The king is on the edge of the board;
(*b*) The king is in check from a rook or a queen;
(*c*) The centre one of the three natural flight squares on the next rank or file is occupied by a defender, usually a pawn;
(*d*) The remaining two squares are controlled by an attacker which may be any man except the rook.

60

A feature of all the above examples excepting one is that mate is delivered by a major piece. Mates by the minor pieces, and even pawns, are not rare but the great majority of all checkmates are delivered by queen or rook. The reason for this is that, as well as giving check, the rook usually commands two of the king's flight squares and the queen any number up to four.

The bishop, on the other hand, only commands one when the king is at the edge of the board, the knight a maximum of one anywhere, and the pawn none at all. It may be useful to summarize these few general hints for forcing checkmate:

(a) Force the enemy king to the edge of the board or in a corner. This is done by a series of checks.

(b) Remember that queen and rook are the easiest pieces with which to mate. If your opponent's king is open to attack, get your queen in close to him.

(c) If you can advance your king with safety, use him to prevent the escape of the enemy king.

61

Let us now go back a move or two in some of these positions and force checkmate.

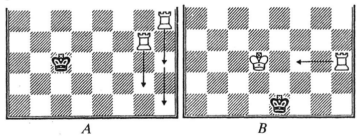

A   B

To start with, consider *A* in relation to 58*C*. Here White forces mate by checking with the rooks in turn. The king is forced to the edge of the board where he is mated. If check is given with the wrong rook, the king escapes briefly but can soon be forced back again (try this and see).

58

A less brutal finish is shown in *B*. White, instead of checking and allowing the king to escape, plays a quiet move to force the black king opposite the white king to reach the mating position in 58*B*. Note that each of the rooks in *A* does the same job in turn that the white king does in *B*: blocking the escape of the black king to the next rank.

62

The next examples give typical play leading to positions similar to those in 59.

A illustrates the idea in 59*A*. White mates by sacrificing

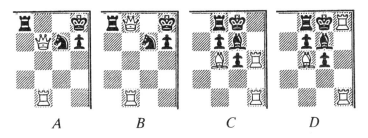

| A | B | C | D |

the queen (*B*). Now the rook must take the queen, when the white rook recaptures to give checkmate. *C* shows another sacrifice. In this position you can see the outlines of 59*F*. White mates by checking with the rook (*D*). The bishop must capture, when the second rook recaptures.

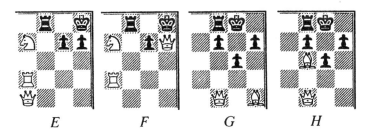

| E | F | G | H |

Note in *E* the pressure of the white pieces around the king. When one side manages to gather a local superiority of strength like this, a direct attack is quite likely to succeed. White plays as in *F* – a queen sacrifice that breaks open the pawn defences. The king must capture, when the rook moves across to mate – the same type of situation as those in 59*G* and *H*:

The end is not hard to see in *G*. White plays as in *H* and now however Black plays he cannot stop the queen giving mate in at most two moves.

You should be able to work this out without difficulty, but if not, look back to 59*D*.

63 *Smothered Mate*

To close our study of mating positions, there is a remarkable finish known as *smothered mate* which is quite often seen. In *A*, the black king is in check and must move

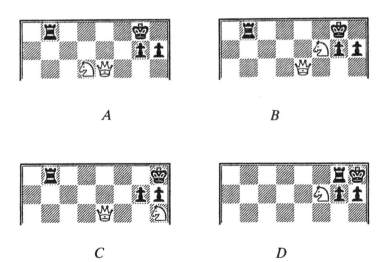

A   B

C   D

into the corner or he is mated at once by the queen (look for this mate). The knight then checks and the king has to move back again (*B*). Now a double check once more drives the king into the corner (*C*). White then makes the spectacular move of placing his queen next to the king to give check – a delightful sacrifice. The king cannot take the queen because she is guarded by the knight (which incidentally is itself attacked!) so the rook must do so, when the knight delivers the 'smothered mate' (*D*).

PART THREE

Strategy

64

The play we have studied so far has been *tactical* – sharp fighting to checkmate or to win material. But many, if not most moves in a game of chess are strategical – *positional* moves as we call them. Put simply, positional play is aimed at improving one's own position or worsening one's opponent's position, which is much the same thing. A good position is one in which the men are strongly posted for attack or defence, work well together and do not get in one another's way. A bad position, of course, is the opposite.

65

Positional play is not an end in itself: it is preparation for tactical play. An attack is likely to succeed only if it starts from a good position. Positional moves aim at making and enlarging weaknesses in the enemy's position and avoiding them in one's own. A weakness may be *temporary* or *permanent*, but is not strictly a weakness unless the other side can take advantage of it – *exploit* it, we say.

66

Positional play is more difficult than tactical play because its aims are less obvious. However, positional play is like tactical play in that there are a number of common situations the correct handling of which can be easily learned. Often both types of play are mixed together, and although positional play is normally preparation for tactical play, sometimes tactical play is for positional advantage.

67   *Force, Space and Time*

A chess game can be said to be of three elements – the men, the board and the moves, often expressed as *force, space* and *time*. If you have the stronger force (in other words, you are ahead in material), you are more likely to win. Similarly, if you control more of the chessboard than your opponent you will again be better placed to win; and lastly, if you have more moves than your opponent then once again you will have the better chances. But, you may wonder, how can I have more moves than my opponent when each of us plays in turn? Think of the initial position of a pawn. Suppose you move it up one square and next play move it again. These two one-step moves might have been achieved by a single two-square jump. You have 'lost' a move (often called a *tempo*). Another example: you advance a piece and it is attacked by a pawn. If you put your man back where it came from you have lost at least one tempo. Beginners frequently waste time like this.

Force, space and time are constant elements in a game of chess but the value of each may vary with the position and the stage of the game. An advantage in force may be matched by the second player's advantage in space for example, but this could be only a temporary balance. Of the three elements, that of material is probably the most important because it is likely to be the more permanent.

If you are a piece ahead, for example, you are more likely to preserve this advantage – perhaps right to the end of the game – than you are to keep an advantage in, say, time.

68
Importance of the Centre

The *centre*, meaning the four central squares and, more loosely, the squares around them (*8*), is most important in chess. The centre is the heart of the chessboard and the main area of battle. From the centre an attack can be turned to left or right much more easily than one can be moved from one side of the board to the other. Control of the centre is usually shared, at least in the early stages of a game. To gain complete control of the centre is often to get a winning advantage.

69

The easiest way to contest the centre is with pawns, and for this reason the usual opening moves for both sides include the advance of one or more of the central pawns. It is not necessary to occupy the centre to contest it however; pieces working from a distance can sometimes do this. To be over-bold in the centre can be as bad as being too timid; however you play though, you must fight for the centre. It is also the best place in which to counter-attack if you are being pressed on one of the wings.

70
Open and Close Positions

There are broadly two kinds of position in the period of preparation for the main battle: the *open* position and the *close* position. In the open position, a pawn or two in the centre have probably been exchanged and the pieces have freedom of movement. Open positions encourage tactical play in which the long-stepping pieces are likely to rule. A close position is one in which few if any pawns have been exchanged and the two sides have either kept apart or have become locked together like boxers who can only jab at each other. Knights enjoy close positions because in them they can move more freely than the other pieces and can take long walks to better squares since the time element is of less importance. Many games, however, are neither wholly open nor wholly closed but share features of both types of position. Pictured are two typical positions early in a game.

Black

Black

A White

B White

A is an open position in which White has control in the centre and so is well placed for attack. *B* is a close position in which chances are about even.

71
The Pawn Structure

We have had to start our study of strategy with a large chunk of theory. Do not worry if you have found this difficult to follow: a few examples will help to make things clearer.

We begin with the pawns because they are very important in positional play. Most weaknesses occur in what we call the *pawn structure* or *pawn skeleton* – the arrangement of the pawns at any particular stage of the game. One reason for this is that no pawn move can be reversed (pawns only go forward, remember) whereas a piece that has been unwisely moved can often be returned to its previous square, even if time is lost. Pawns alone are usually strongest when they stand next to one another on a

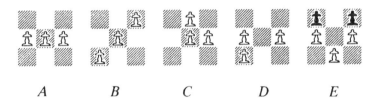

A   B   C   D   E

rank (*A*), and often when they are defending one another in a diagonal line (*B*), particularly when the line points towards the centre of the board. Pawns are a little weaker where a pair is *doubled* on a file (as in *C*) and much weaker when *doubled* and *isolated* (*D*). An isolated pawn is one that has no friendly pawn on a next-door file. A pawn may be *backward*, like the central white pawn in *E*. A backward pawn also cannot be supported by a friendly pawn but for a different reason: its advance is prevented by an enemy man, usually a pawn, that occupies or attacks a square in its path.

A pawn weakness need only be temporary: in *D* for example, a capture by the pawn on the dark square would regain the ideal formation shown in *A*.

72

When a pawn is attacked by an enemy piece – a common happening – it may not be possible or convenient to guard it with a friendly man. Under these circumstances the only defence may be to advance the attacked pawn. Look at *A*:

here a rook attacks doubled and isolated pawns. The weakness of these pawns is obvious: they cannot defend each other and are unable to escape the rook's attack. Two pawns side-by-side are much better placed, as the sequence *B–E* shows. In *B*, the rook attacks one pawn that moves forward a square and is then protected by the other (*C*). The rook attacks the second pawn (*D*), which moves up two squares so as to be defended by its companion (*E*). Now the rook can return to attack the first pawn which can no longer be defended. When the pawn is captured, however, the second pawn will already have reached the fifth rank and, depending on the position elsewhere on the board, may prove dangerous as it is near to promotion.

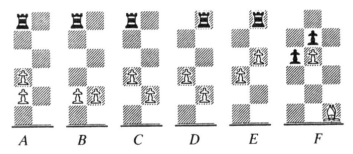

In *F*, Black has a *passed* pawn. A passed pawn is one that cannot be stopped by an opposing pawn and may be thought of as the opposite of a backward pawn. A backward pawn is weak, but a passed pawn, particularly if defended as here, is strong because the other side must employ a piece to stop its advance. If, in *F*, the white bishop moves away the passed pawn may race to queen.

73 *Protecting the King*
Squares controlled by pawns cannot be occupied by pieces

of the opposite colour without material loss. As far as possible, therefore, pawns should be used to control squares on which enemy pieces would be well placed – particularly in the centre and around the kings' positions. Pawns in defence are usually strongest if unmoved. It is necessary to protect your king with pawns, and *A–E* show good defences for a castled king, particularly in open or half-open positions (in close positions there may be less danger to the king).

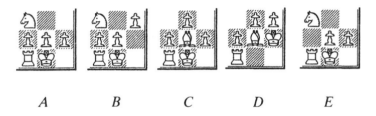

A   B   C   D   E

A is the normal position after king's side castling; *B* shows a slight weakening of the pawn structure, but against this there is now an escape square for the king off the back rank (remember the lesson of 59*A*!). *C* is strong but is weak without the bishop, as all the pawns are on dark squares which means that the light squares could be well used by the enemy (look back to 62*H*). *D* combines the ideas in *B* and *C*. *E* is good for attack (as the rook has an open line) but a little weaker for defence because there are only two pawns to shield the king.

74

A pawn in the centre is worth more than one at the side, at least during the main battle. From this you will understand that when you have a choice of pawns for a capture it is better to take with the one farthest from the middle because it will then be brought one file nearer. *A* and *B* show this.

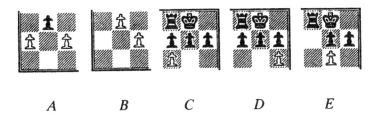

A   B   C   D   E

Pawns in attack can be used to destroy the king's fortress and open lines for the pieces to work on. A sacrifice is often the best way to do this. *C*, *D* and *E* are examples. In each case, Black's defence position is weakened whether or not the pawn is captured.

75   *The Queen*

The pawns have claimed our attention so far. Let us now look at the pieces in turn and see how each can be used to best advantage.

The queen is at her best on an open board, especially when the enemy forces are scattered and unprotected. In the early part of the game the queen plays only a modest part, and that at a safe distance from the close fighting. The queen's weakness is that, being the best piece, she must move if attacked.

Do not bring the queen out too early for your opponent may then gain time by attacking her whilst developing his own pieces. Do not exchange your queen if you have the weaker force: she may later be able to worry the enemy king, for as we saw earlier the queen is the easiest piece with which to mate.

69

76

Rooks like *open files* to work on. Open files are files without pawns on them.

Rooks that are doubled on an open file can prove very strong, particularly if in the centre or near the enemy king. Make open files for your rooks by exchanging pawns. The rook does not work well on the ranks with one exception – the seventh rank, where the opponent's pawns stand at the start of a game. Here the rook is at its best for it can:

    (*a*) Attack unmoved pawns, itself free from pawn attack;

    (*b*) Confine the enemy king to the edge of the board.

In *A* you will see that a rook on the seventh can tie down enemy pieces to the defence of pawns. *B* shows one way of challenging this threat: if the white rook checks,

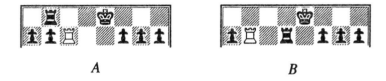

        A   *B*

the king moves up and Black's pawns are secure. *C–F* demonstrate the power of a rook on the seventh coupled with a discovered check – a marriage of the positional and the tactical. White uncovers a check with a capture, forcing the king to move (*D*) and then returns to drive the king into the corner (*E*) and repeat the slaughter (*F*). All Black's queen's side men are lost in this way, including the queen.

        C   *D*

E   F

It is a good principle not to put your rook in front of your pawns, for here it will be open to attack and may also get in the way of a pawn which you wish to advance. The rook is a long-range piece and is best placed at the back of your army until later in the game or until it can be played with safety to the seventh rank.

77 *The Bishops*

The minor pieces are the real workers of the game. The bishop is active from the start but, like the major pieces, prefers open lines.

The peculiar feature of the bishop is its 'one-colour' move. A bishop's freedom is limited if 'friendly' pawns occupy many of the same-coloured squares: bishops are sometimes reduced to doing the work of pawns!

A shows a bishop on the same-coloured squares as the pawns. White controls less than half of the mini-board and black pieces can walk freely on the light squares.

By contrast, a bishop on the opposite-coloured squares has freedom of movement and works well with friendly

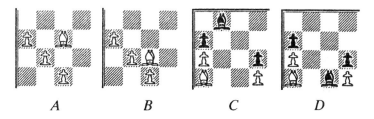

A   B   C   D

pawns – compare *B*, where the white men control nearly twice as many squares.

It is common, for reasons we need not discuss, for a player in the course of a game to get most of his pawns on the squares of one colour. It is also common for the other player to have most of his pawns on the squares of the opposite colour. The bishop that is then best for defence (as in *B*) is also best for attack since it is on the same colour as most of the opposing pawns. This is called the *good bishop* and its companion the *bad bishop*. *C* illustrates a good bishop (the white one) and a bad bishop.

If you are left with a bad bishop, it is better to post it in front of the pawns (*D*) rather than behind (*C*), for here at least it has more space. A bad bishop, as in these examples, is often tied to defence whilst a good bishop can move about looking for targets and can also choose the moment to attack them. This small study would be of little importance if both sides kept both bishops throughout a game, but this rarely happens. Each time a bishop of either side can be exchanged you have to consider whether it is, or will become, a good or bad bishop, and act accordingly. These are easy words, and on a crowded board and in the heat of the battle it is easy to over-look this important positional factor.

78 *The Knights*

The knight, because of its short step and the ease with which it can move on a crowded board, is most valuable in the early and middle stages of a game when there are many pawns about. As these are exchanged or captured the long-moving pieces become stronger and the knights, because of this, weaker. A knight posted in the centre where it is also free from attack by enemy pawns is very strong. Knights at the side of the board are weak because they attack less squares (22) and do not bear on the central position.

Knights are equally useful in attack and defence, but you should avoid moving them about looking for victims just because they have an interesting move or in the hope that their sly threats may be overlooked.

79 *The King*

The king must be kept in safety for most of the game. The best way to do this is to castle and then to make as few pawn moves in front of the king as necessary. King's-side castling is more common than queen's-side castling because it can be achieved quicker (there is one piece less to move off the back line) and because the king then defends the wing pawn which it does not on the queen's side. When most of the pieces have gone from the board and there is little risk of checkmate the king can come out of hiding. What is more, he can prove a very useful piece; for example, as a companion for a pawn marching towards promotion or as an executioner amongst the enemy pawns. At close range, a king is stronger than any other piece except the queen and he should be used to take advantage of this.

80 *Exchanging Men*

Several times we have talked about 'exchanging' – taking an enemy man for the loss of one of our men of equal value (a pawn for a pawn, a bishop for a knight). Opportunities for exchanging are likely to arise many times in a game and it is natural to ask whether it is good or bad to 'exchange'. The answer depends on the position.

A good first rule is that if you are ahead in material or under heavy attack you should try to exchange; if behind, or you are attacking, you should avoid exchanges, particularly of the queens.

Here are other things you should think about.

(*a*) Exchanges usually favour one side or the other, even if only slightly. Consider the men to be exchanged, particularly if a bishop is involved (77). Which man is better placed or is likely to become stronger (you have to think ahead here)?

(*b*) Will the position of a man that makes the recapture be better or worse afterwards?

(*c*) Will the exchange still be possible next move (it may be better to delay it)?

(*d*) Would it be in your favour if your opponent captured first, and if so, can you make him do so?

These questions are not too difficult to answer where the men to be exchanged are similar. It is much more difficult to decide whether a bishop should be exchanged for a knight, or perhaps a queen and pawn for two rooks. Here you need especially to consider the pieces' positional values which we have been discussing. These values, remember, take large account of the pawn structure.

81

Here now are two positions which we will discuss in general terms only.

White is a piece behind in *A* yet will win because of his big positional advantage. White has most space and is in command of the two open files. The white minor pieces are well placed and the advanced pawns cramp the black position. Notice how White controls all the dark-square 'holes' in the centre and on the king's side. If you look closely at the black position you will see that no man can move without loss. This is an extreme case to show clearly

A   B

what is meant by a 'positional advantage' – Black in fact is in 'zugzwang' (31).

By contrast, *B* is an ordinary position from an ordinary game. Let us make a quick assessment of this position. Black is a pawn ahead in material; has a well-placed knight in the centre which is secure from pawn attack; a queen's side pawn majority (making it easier to get a passed pawn on this side); a 'good' bishop, though inactive at present, and a safe king position. White's knight is also well placed; he has a good line of attack for his king's rook, and he is threatening either to break up the pawns on Black's queen's side or to get a rook to the seventh rank after exchanging pawns. Like Black, his king's position is safe at present. White is attacking but Black can also find interesting play – for example, by striking at White's central pawn. Verdict: a fairly level game, depending on whose turn it is to move.

Try to look at your games like this. In every position there are signposts that should give you ideas that will help you to find the right, or at least a good move. If you read only a few of these signposts your play will rapidly

75

improve.

82 *Judgment*

You now have an insight into the elements of both tactical and positional play. However, if chess was only a matter of applying correctly the simple principles we have been looking at, it would be a dull game. But chess is never dull. At each move the players are faced with a new situation in which there will probably be several good, or good-looking moves, positional or tactical or both. So at each turn the players must make a decision – which move is best? This is the hardest part of the game – we call it *judgment*. Sound judgment comes with experience. In your games you should try to see one or two moves ahead in those lines of play you think are important (not every line: you would need a computer to do that!).

Looking ahead means not only planning your own moves but also foreseeing the moves your opponent may make in reply. Do not spend much time on this. It is usually better not to attempt to work out moves accurately except where you think a combination is forced; that is, where one or both sides must follow a certain line of play to avoid loss. Instead, try to look at your game as we examined the positions above – in general terms only. This should help you find a plan and from it your move. Anyone who says 'I don't know what to do now' (and someone is always saying it!) is just not thinking.

PART FOUR
Scoring

83

It is a feature of chess that games and positions can be simply and briefly recorded. This is of great value for it means that we can learn from and enjoy the games of the experts and also keep a record of our own games. A record of a game is called a *game score* or simply a *score.*

There are several scoring systems, or *notations* as they are usually called, but only three are common. The ALGEBRAIC and the DESCRIPTIVE are used for recording games whilst the FORSYTH is used for recording positions. The Algebraic is in general use. The Descriptive is falling from favour but is standard in old books.

When studied for the first time these systems may seem difficult and confusing, but they are really neither and you will be surprised how quickly you are able to use them.

84

We will examine the Algebraic and Descriptive notations together for they have much in common. If you later want to keep a record of your games you can then decide which system you prefer. The Algebraic will be used for the rest of this book.

85

Notations describe chess moves accurately and as briefly

as possible. The elements of a move are two:

(*a*) The man moved;

(*b*) The square to which the man is moved.

It is enough to record these: there is normally no need to describe also the square on which the man stands before the move.

Both the Algebraic and the Descriptive identify the men by initial letters:

K – king	Q – queen	R – rook
B – bishop	N or Kt – knight	P – pawn

(A further economy is practised in the Algebraic: the P initial is dropped, it being understood that a move which is not prefixed by a capital letter is a pawn move. Symbols, as used in diagrams, now frequently replace initial letters in books and magazines.)

The two systems differ, however, in their description of the squares.

86

In the Algebraic notation the files of the chessboard are lettered 'a' to 'h' from left to right and the ranks from 1 to 8 from bottom to top *as seen from White's side of the board*. A square is described by its file and rank designation in that order. For example, the bottom left square is a1 (see diagram). Note that each square has a unique description.

In the Descriptive notation, the *files are named after the pieces standing on them in the initial position*. Pieces on the king's side are called after the king (king's rook, king's knight, king's bishop) and those on the queen's side are similarly called after the queen. Notice that the file decriptions are the same for White and Black. The ranks are numbered 1 to 8 *from each side*. White's second rank, for example, is Black's seventh rank (see diagram).

A square is described by file and rank, in that order. So each square has two names, one read from the White side of the board and the other from the Black side (it may help you to turn the diagram round to see this).

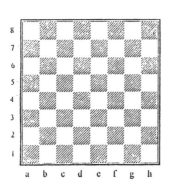

ALGEBRAIC NOTATION

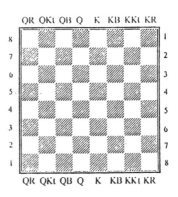

DESCRIPTIVE NOTATION

White's K1, for example, is Black's K8; White's QKt4 is the same square as Black's QKt5, and so on. Notice again that the file description is the same for both sides and that the sum of the ranks reckoned from each side adds up to nine (thus your third rank is your opponent's sixth, etc.).

87

A move is recorded in both systems by the symbol for the man moved, followed by a hyphen (usually omitted in the Algebraic) and the symbol for the square to which the move is made. In the Descriptive notation *a White move is always recorded from White's side of the board and a Black move from Black's side of the board.* Let us suppose that both players move their kings one square up the file from the initial position. Both White and Black moves would be described as K–K2 in the Descriptive notation and would be written down like this by both players; in the Algebraic notation, the White move would be described as Ke2 and the Black move as Ke7 and both players would write the moves down in this way.

88

Notation is chess shorthand, and like shorthand it should be as brief and clear as possible. Often two similar men of the same colour can move to the same square, so it is necessary to indicate which man is moved. This is done in the Algebraic by indicating *either* the rank *or* the file on which the man stands. For example, if you had a rook on a1 and the other on a3, and you wanted to move the one in the corner to a2, the move would be described as R1a2. If you had rooks on a1 and c1 and you wanted to move the one in the corner to b1, the move would be recorded as Rab1. With rooks on a1 and c3 and you wished to advance the corner rook to a3, you could record this either as Raa3 or as R1a3. Look back to (74)A&B for an example of a pawn capture. This would be recorded as axb3.

With the Descriptive notation, the same principle is applied: the square on which the piece stands is indicated immediately after the piece symbol. See diagram D in (90) for an example.

89
Notation Symbols

A capture is shown in both notations by an 'x' (sometimes, in the Algebraic only, by a colon). This is followed in the Algebraic by the square on which the capture is made and in the Descriptive by the symbol for the man captured.

Other symbols used in one or both notations are given opposite.

Scoring

Symbol	Meaning	Symbol	Meaning
–(hyphen)	to	0–0 (or)	Castles
x (or) :	takes	Castles (K)	king's side
+ (or) ch.	check		
‡ (or) mate	checkmate	0–0–0 (or)	Castles
		Castles (Q)	queen's side
(Q) [or]	Promotion to	e.p.	en passant
(= Q)	queen (after	!	good move
	pawn move)		
dis. ch.	discovered	?	bad move
	check	! ?	move that
dbl. ch.	double check		may be good or bad

90

Below is the end of a game, shown move by move, in which both the Algebraic and Descriptive notations (in **bold** type) are used for comparison. All the types of moves that may give difficulty in scoring are included. Also, the game is a good example of complicated tactical play. Comments cover both recording of moves and the purpose of the moves in the game.

A – Black to Play

(Black Moves)

B – Qf7 **Q–KB2**

A – Black is to play in this position. White is threatening to win a rook for nothing by moving the knight away to give a discovered check.

B – Black moves the queen. Notice that Q–B2 would not be a sufficient description as the queen could also have moved to QB2. Now White has no discovered check and Black is attacking the bishop with his queen.

(White Moves)
C – 0–0 **Castles**

(Black Moves)
D – Rb × d5
R(Kt4) × Kt

C – White defends the bishop by castling. This move would only be allowed if the king and rook had not moved previously. White is now in a position to uncover an attack on the queen by moving the bishop.

D – Black captures the knight with a rook, hoping to win two minor pieces for a rook. As the capture could have been made by either black rook, you should note carefully how the move is recorded in each notation.

E – White surprisingly does not recapture the rook but plays on the pawn which is now only one square off promotion. Only one pawn can move to R7, so there is no need to describe this move as 'P–QR7'.

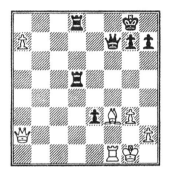

(White Moves)
E – a7 **P–R7**

(Black Moves)
F – e2 **P–K7**

F – Black counter-attacks, threatening the white rook.

(White Moves)
G – B × e2 **B × P**

(Black Moves)
H – Rf5 **R–KB4**

G – White could easily have made a bad move here: if he had taken the pawn with the queen instead of with the bishop, Black would have been able to capture White's advanced pawn with a check (look at this – it is not easy to see). Calamitous for White would have been Bxd5 (instead of Bxe2) when Black would have had the crushing reply xf1(Q) mate. Instead of the move played, White could also have won with the clever sacrifice Qxd5!

H – As this rook can move also to QB4, the description 'R–B4' is not sufficient. Notice the black queen is now pinned and the white queen is 'en prise'.

(White Moves)
I – a8(Q) **P–R8 (=Q)**

(Black Moves)
J – R × f1 ch **R × Rch**

I – White promotes the pawn and now has two queens on the board (a rook can be turned upside down to represent a second queen during a game).

J – Here, as in *D* and *G*, the Descriptive notation shows the man captured, and the Algebraic the square on which the capture is made.

(White Moves)
K – B × f1   **B × R**

(Black Moves)
L – R × a8   **R × Q**

(White Moves)
M – Q × a8 ch   **Q × Rch.**

(Black Moves)
N – Qf8   **Q–B1**

O – In the Descriptive notation when a side has only one bishop left, the simple move description 'B–B4' is always correct since the bishop could never play to KB4 and QB4 or any other matched pair of squares as these are always of opposite colours. Discovery of chessboard facts like this will widen your understanding and help you to

(White Moves)
O – Bc4ch **B–B4ch.**

(Black Moves)
P – Kh8 **K–R1**

play the game better.

P – The king has been forced away from protection of the queen which is again pinned. A 'back rank' mate, such as we saw in 62*B* follows.

(White Moves)
Q – Q × f8 mate **Q × Q mate**

91
The FORSYTH is a quick and accurate way of recording

positions (useful, for example, when a game has to be broken off). Unoccupied squares are indicated by the appropriate number and the men by the usual abbreviations, capital letters for the white men and small letters for the black men.

Starting at the top left of the chessboard seen from White's side (square a8) each rank in turn is recorded from left to right, ending with the bottom right-hand square (h1). Ranks are divided by strokes but two or more empty ranks may be grouped together. Chessmen and square numbers should of course add up to 64! The final position above (Q) would be recorded in Forsyth as:

5Q1k / 6pp / 16 / 2B5 / 6P1 / 7P / 6K1

PART FIVE

Playing the Game

92

You now have a fair idea of the peculiarities of the different men and how they behave in attack and defence, and you also know the differences between positional and tactical play. Before we begin a proper game, however, we need to know how to apply our knowledge so that our moves may have purpose from the start.

93

Let us follow a game through in outline without making moves. At the beginning, only the knights and pawns can move so our first task is to give our other pieces freedom and then to get them on to good squares for both attack and defence. A good square may be described as one on which a man is well placed to take part in the coming battle, and where he has *mobility*, or freedom of movement. A man's mobility may be limited by enemy men who oppose it or by friendly men who get in its way, or both. A good square for one man (a knight, for example) will probably be a bad square for another man (say a rook) because different men command different squares. This early part of the game, when the first task of each side is to 'get the pieces out' or *develop* them (both terms are well used) is called the OPENING. The next stage, that of the battle proper, is known as the MIDDLE GAME. There is no clear division between the opening and the middle game.

94

In the middle game, your plans should be directed towards making and attacking weak points in your opponent's position and avoiding or defending weaknesses in your own position. Each move you make is therefore either an attacking move or a defensive move, or often a move that is part attacking, part defensive. An attacking move is often the best defensive move anyway because in chess, as in many other games, attack is one of the best forms of defence. If you become a good chessplayer you will find that there is never time for an idle and pointless move.

95

After the middle game, when the big battle has died down, comes the END GAME. In the end game, the kings are usually out of direct danger because there are few men left on the board. Pawn promotion is often the main aim of each side in an end game. Opening, middle game and end game are merely terms used to describe three different stages of the game, but a game of chess remains a whole – a single, continuous fight from start to finish.

96

We are now ready to play through the score of an actual game. The moves of a game are numbered progressively and each number covers a move by both players. If we wish to talk about a particular move it is necessary to state who made it; for example, White's seventh move, Black's eighteenth.

The game given is between strong players and contains

many examples of play that we have studied. Follow the game through on a board and check with the diagrams that you are doing this correctly. Set up the men in the initial position (5) – dark squares left-hand corner, remember! White always moves first.

	White	Black
1.	e4	c6
2.	d4	d5
3.	exd5	cxd5

Both players have been fighting for control of the centre which is for the moment shared. It is also locked – neither central pawn can move.

4.	c4

The opening is given its character by this move. An expert will tell you that this is the Panov–Botvinnik attack in the Caro–Kann defence – chess often sounds more difficult than it is!

4.	. . .	Nf6
5.	Nc3	e6
6.	Nf3	Nc6

Both players activate their unmoved knights.

7.	Bd3	dxc4
8.	Bxc4	Be7

Some interesting things have been happening. After White had developed his king's bishop, Black exchanged pawns, making White move the bishop again. White could

90

not long delay moving this bishop because he needs to castle, but equally he did not want himself to exchange pawns, perhaps because he saw it would free the black queen's bishop which is at present shut in and lacks mobility. Now White has an isolated pawn in the centre, but since it is on the fourth rank whilst Black's centre pawn is on the third and cannot advance to the fourth without loss, White has more space in the centre to make up for the isolation of his pawn. The plans of both sides are based on this central pawn position. Black will play to bring his forces to attack the isolated pawn which he hopes will prove a weakness to White, whilst his opponent

Position after Black's 8th
move

Position after White's 11th
move

intends to make use of his greater freedom in the middle and the fact that Black's QB is shut in to prepare an attack against the king. Both sides are continuing to develop their pieces. Check your position now with the diagram.

| 9. | 0–0 | 0–0 |
| 10. | Re1 | a6 |

Black's last move is a common manoeuvre. He prepares to advance his b-pawn gaining space on the queen's side, forcing the white bishop to move again and also allowing the black bishop to get to b7 where it will bear down on the light-coloured squares in the centre. White's next move is the usual counter to this idea (check your position against the diagram). Let us see what might then happen if Black continued with his plan (this is not part of the game remember!) 11. a4, b5?; 12. axb5, axb5?; 13. Rxa8, and White is winning.

| 11. | a4 | Qd6 |
| 12. | Be3 | Rd8 |

The threat to White's isolated centre pawn is building up. Black has three pieces attacking it now: notice that the rook behind the queen is one of these although it does not directly threaten the pawn.

| 13. | Qe2 | Bd7 |
| 14. | Rad1 | |

Now, suddenly, White has achieved an almost ideal position; all his pieces bear on the centre and are on good squares and the king is in safety. The black pieces are not so happy. The two bishops are lazy and the queen is awkwardly placed. Black suffers from too little room to move about so that his pieces are in one another's way. White has gained in space. However, Black's disadvantage may only prove temporary and at present he has no permanent weaknesses in his position (see diagram on p. 94).

| 14. | . . | Nb4 |

Playing the Game

As the white d-pawn is isolated, d5 is an ideal square for a knight, as we have seen (78). Black plans to take advantage of this but if he moves the KKt at once to d5, White will be able to exchange it and Black will be obliged to retake with the pawn when he will have failed in his aim of achieving a positional strong-point. The move played will allow him to secure a knight at d5.

15.   Ne5

White's knight moves directly to a good central square and also frees the f-pawn to advance if necessary.

15.	. . .	Nbd5
16.	Nxd5	Nxd5
17.	Qh5	

Now White starts the attack on the king's position and threatens to take off the bishop's pawn which is twice attacked (by the knight and the queen) and only once defended (by the king). Notice that White could not have played his last move if he had not exchanged knights the move before as the black knight was guarding the square the white queen now occupies. White does not wish to exchange his bishop for the remaining black knight as he plans to use it to attack the light-coloured squares around the enemy king.

| 17. | . . . | Be8 |
| 18. | Bd3 | |

The black bishop has been forced back in defence and now White threatens to checkmate in two moves. (Can you see this? If Black does not take action, White will play

Qxh7 ch followed by Qh8 mate.) This is not the purpose of White's move however, for he cannot expect his opponent to overlook the danger. The plan involves the sacrifice of a pawn which will signal an all-out attack on the black king.

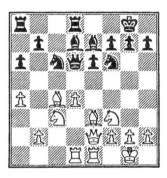

Position after White's
14th move

Position after White's
17th move

18. ...   Nf6

It may surprise you that this strong-looking move probably loses the game. Correct was 18. ... f5; uncovering an attack on the queen and shutting out the dangerous white bishop.

19. Qh4   Bxa4

The white queen would be attacked if the black knight moved – a 'discovered attack' – but she is safe for the moment as a knight move would allow either the mate mentioned above or the capture of the knight by the queen. Look at each of the five possible moves by this knight and satisfy yourself that this is correct.

Black decides to take the pawn White has sacrificed, but this loses an important tempo and removes one of the only two pieces defending the king. Black now has two pawns to one on the queen's side and hopes to win in the end game after stopping the attack on his king.

20.	Rd2	Bb5
21.	Bb1	g6

Some more interesting play. Black was prepared, on his 20th move, to allow his extra pawn to be doubled and isolated in order to get rid of the white bishop, but White wisely keeps the piece by moving it away.

Black now tries to block the attack by moving up his g-pawn, but this creates a weakness on the dark squares round the king (compare 59*D*). Now White's other bishop becomes dangerous as a result. Black could have stopped White's next move by 21. . . . h6 (instead of 21. . . . g6) but then White would have had the bright sacrifice 22. Bxh6!, breaking open the defence.

If Black then accepted the sacrifice (22. . . . gxh6) White would have continued 23. Qxh6!, and since the black knight would still have been unable to move because of the mate starting with Qh7 ch, there would have been no good answer to the White threat of Re3 followed by Rg3. You are probably bewildered by these possibilities, but it is enough if you have noticed how weak a king who has lost his pawn defence can be.

22.	Bg5	Nd5

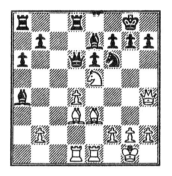

Position after Black's
19th move

Position after Black's
22nd move

The white move attacked the knight twice and it was only once defended. Black moves the knight so that the bishop is defended twice (necessary, as it is now twice attacked). However, the knight has been forced away from the defence of the king's position where White now has several pieces concentrated: White is ready to strike! Black could have defended the knight instead of moving it by the move 22. . . . Kg7; but this would also have lost although the play is rather too complicated to go into here.

| 23. | Nxf7 | Kxf7 |
| 24. | Qxh7 ch | Ke8 |

Black had to take the offered knight. If instead he had tried 23. . . . Bxg5; White would have continued 24. Nxg5 and there would have been two white pieces attacking both the rook's pawn and the king's pawn, each of which would have been only once defended – a double attack which could not have been met. White would then have been a pawn ahead in material and the black king without shelter – a hopeless situation in a game between strong players.

25.	Bxg6 ch	Kd7
26.	Rxe6!	

Another sacrifice! White now has three pawns for the knight and so is level in material, but Black is desperately placed. He cannot take the rook with either king or queen. Notice 26. . . . Kxe6? 27. Bf5, a curious mid-board checkmate. Also after 26. . . . Qxe6; again 27. Bf5 and the Black queen is pinned and lost for the bishop. After this exchange (queen for bishop) the point count on each side would be White 22, Black 21. Only a one-point advantage, but White would control most space, the black pieces would be tied to the defence of the king – a real danger of checkmate exists in this sort of position – and White would probably be able to promote one of his king's-side pawns without difficulty.

26.	. . .	Qb4
27.	Bf5	Kc7

Black must escape the terrible 'discovered check' that is threatened (see 44).

28.	Bxe7	Qxd2

Black allows a discovered check. He could have retaken the bishop with the knight (28. . . . Nxe7) but after White's 29. Rxe7 ch, the end would not have been far off. Follow through this possible finish: 28. . . . Nxe7 (instead

Position after White's 26th   Final position
move

of 28. . . . Qxd2); 29. Rxe7 ch, Kb6; 30. Rxb7 ch, Ka5;
31. Qc7 ch, Ka4; 32. Bc2 ch, Qb3; 33. Qc3 and White will
mate next move however Black plays. (Work this out: not
all the replies are easy to see.) This is a good example of
what is called a 'king hunt'. However, these are all dreams,
for Black decided to take the unguarded White rook. You
can recover the game position from the diagram.

29. Bd6 dbl ch

At this point Black gives up the game. Because White's
last move was a double check, the black king would have to
move. He has three squares to choose from; let's see what
would then happen in each case.

(a) 29. . . . Kc6; 30. Bc5 dis ch, Rd6; 31. Rxd6 mate.

(b) 29. . . . Kc8; 30. Re8 dis ch, Bd7; 31. Q(or B) xd7
mate.

(c) 29. . . . Kb6 (best); 30. Bb4 dis ch, Bc6; 31. Bxd2,
and now Black, nine points behind in material, is
soon lost.

98

97

Of course this game was difficult for you to follow and you will not be able to think and play like this for a long time. The game was an exciting one though, and did show clearly several useful things: the early fight for the centre and how the plans of each side grew from it, an attack on the king's position where the attacking force was better placed and stronger than the defending force, the sacrifice to break down the pawn defence and the king chase that followed. The game did not reach an end game proper for there were still many pieces on the board at the surrender.

98

When you start playing yourself you will make many mistakes – not just little mistakes (you will make these most of the time!) but big mistakes, like putting your queen 'en prise' or allowing your king to be mated when you are not looking. You will make big positional mistakes too, though they will not be so obvious. But all these mistakes will be steps to knowledge and you will soon find that you make less and less bad mistakes and you will then be able to pay more attention to the smaller mistakes. Win or lose, though, the game is the thing – and if you forget chess is a game it is better to forget chess.

99 *Planning*

When you play chess, always have a plan. At the start of a game, your plan will probably be to get your pieces on to good squares and, if possible, to capture the centre. Be ready to change your plan, however, if your opponent makes what you think is a bad mistake. In the middle game you may develop a bold plan, such as a direct attack on the king as White carried out in the above game, or a less ambitious and perhaps better plan of securing some positional advantage – a rook on the seventh rank perhaps, a well-posted knight or a strong pawn centre. At each move you will have to consider whether your plan is still the best one – this is where judgment comes in. Do not be afraid to change your plan – in fact, you will need to change it, perhaps many times in the course of a game. A plan is based on the position and takes account of all the men on both sides. Do not be tempted to make a move which is not part of your plan unless you think the move is necessary. It is a common failing to make a move that is not part of a general plan, and perhaps is even without reason. At best, such moves are wasted but more often they are simply bad.

100 *Resigning*

In conclusion, let us see the various ways in which a game can end. We have already met three: checkmate, stalemate, and by surrender, as in the above game. We talk of the player who gives up as RESIGNING the game. It is right to resign a game in which no chance remains for this saves time and is also polite. However, what makes up a hopeless position will depend on the strength of the players and it is best, when starting to play, to carry on until checkmate. Another way to end the game has nothing to do with the position on the board. When a time limit is set on the number of moves that each side must make, and this is usual in match play, then a player who oversteps this limit loses the game.

101 *Drawn Game*

In the same way that one player can resign, so can both players agree a DRAW at any time during the game; one player offers, the other accepts and the game is over. This is the usual manner in which a draw is reached but there are several other ways.

(*a*) *Insufficient Force*
Neither side is strong enough to force mate. An obvious example is where each side is left with just a king. This will be explained more fully later.

(*b*) *Perpetual Check*
A position is sometimes reached where one side can force a continuous series of checks – a sort of see-saw or merry-go-round. Here are three examples:

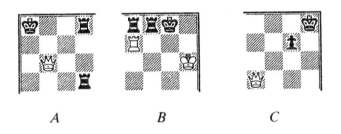

A   B   C

In *A*, after 1. Qa6 ch, Kb8; 2. Qb6 ch, Kc8; 3. Qc6 ch, the king must go back again. In *B*, play could go 1. Rg7 ch, Kh8; 2. Rh7 ch, Kg8; for ever. In *C*, after 1. Qe8 ch, Kh7; 2. Qh5 ch, Kg8; these moves can be repeated indefinitely. White could equally have played 1. Qh5 ch, for the same result. A player who is otherwise losing will be happy to force a perpetual check; a player who is winning will seek to avoid it.

(*c*) *Repeated Position*
If the identical position occurs three times in a game with the same player to move, a draw may be claimed by either player. A perpetual check is one kind of repeated position.

101

(d) *Fifty-move Rule*

This is a very rare finish. Where both sides have made fifty consecutive moves without a pawn being played or a capture made, either side may claim a draw. In certain specified positions, the number of moves is increased.

PART SIX

The Openings

102

We have seen that a game of chess always starts from the same position, called the *initial position*. In this position there are a half-dozen starting moves for White which are considered good. In reply to each of these, Black has three or four good replies when again White usually has a number of possibilities – and so on. These are the OPENINGS – the play of both sides at the beginning of a game in which the players are repeating (whether they know it or not) moves that have been played many times before. Within these well-tried and named openings there will be secondary lines many of which may also have names. These names are useful only for discussion and reference. If, for example, the 'Giuoco Piano' (to give one of the commonest) is mentioned, most chess-players will know at once the first three moves of each side.

103

You need know very little about the openings to play chess reasonably well, for they are only series of moves based on the principles of strategy and tactics we have already studied. It is much more important to know what you are trying to do in the opening, and how to do it, than to learn by heart sequences of moves which you do not really understand.

104

Defeat can come quickly in the opening if you sin against principles. The shortest game of chess is only two moves long and is known, rather unfairly as it is not obvious, as Fool's Mate. White ignores the centre and development and instead moves wing pawns that bare his king.

	White	Black
1.	g4	e5 (or e6)
2.	f3 (or f4)	Qh4 mate

There is an attack much favoured by beginners that can also come to a quick end. This example is known as Scholar's Mate.

	White	Black
1.	e4	e5
2.	Bc4	Bc5
3.	Qf3 (or h5)	Nc6
4.	Qxf7 mate	

White's play, although successful here, was not good because the queen was brought out too early, which is a positional mistake (75). Also, the attack relied on Black overlooking the threat to the bishop's pawn (he could have played 3. . . . Qe7). Do not make a move or a combination whose success depends on your opponent not seeing your plan: this is bad chess. It is certain that you will face several attempts to bluff you with this attack so make sure you understand how to defend against it.

Game 1: Final Position   Game 2: Final Position

105
Main Aims

It would be nice if we could reduce all the openings to a few general rules of play; this however is not possible, for whilst some openings are straightforward, others are hugely difficult. Again, some offer plenty of tactical play, even in the first few moves, others little or none. But there are a few features that are common to most openings and these deserve our special study. Two aims stand out from the rest: to get one's pieces on to good squares and to strike at the centre. We have already explained their importance. If you follow these guides alone you will not play the openings badly. However, there is one useful study which will also serve you well as it is difficult to think of an opening in which it may not occur: the pin of a knight by a bishop.

106
Opening Pins

It is enough that you know the objects of each side in this small battle within a battle, and the usual alternatives that may be available. An understanding of these will lead you to the correct way to deal with less common positions.

Each knight on its first play may have a choice of up to three squares to which to move. Let us take, as an example, White's QN. One square is at the edge of the board (a3), and two are towards the centre (c3 and d2). The move away from the centre (Na3) is almost always bad, and of the other two, Nc3, which strikes at two central squares, is usually best. However, a knight whose initial move is to the c- or f-file can often be pinned against the king or queen respectively. The pin of a knight by a bishop under these circumstances can favour the attacker in several small ways:

(a) The move develops a piece (the bishop);
(b) The pin at once stops an enemy piece (the knight) from moving and temporarily destroys its powers;
(c) The pin often hinders enemy development;
(d) The attack frequently threatens to gain a positional advantage, and sometimes to win material. For this reason the pin may compel a reply which is defensive or otherwise not the best.

Against these advantages must be set the fact that the pin often threatens nothing or makes only a temporary weakness in the enemy position. The bishop may then be driven away or forced to take the knight, in both cases with probable loss of time. In sum, the pin is often, but by no means always good.

107

Let us look first at the most serious threat: gain of material. Here the idea is the same that we saw in 47 D. If the knight can be attacked with a pawn, the piece may be lost. A shows part of an opening position. The knight cannot be saved. A more common position, which at first sight also loses a piece, is shown in B. Notice the difference between *A* and *B*. Now Black, to play, can save the piece at the cost of a pawn by attacking the bishop (*C*).

A   B   C

If the bishop moves back to keep the pin, Black attacks it again with the knight's pawn. However White plays he cannot do better than win a pawn. Positions similar to these will recur many times in your openings: look closely at them!

108

Consider now the two types of opening pin; against the king where the knight cannot legally move, and against the queen where it may move but probably only at great loss (*A*). White would not wish to capture the king's knight in *A* because this would help Black's development and leave his pawns undisturbed.

A   B

The position is different on the queen's side. If the bishop took the knight here, Black would be forced to double his pawns and isolate his rook's pawn, thereby making weaknesses in the pawn structure (71). The exchange would favour Black, however, in that a pawn would be brought nearer the centre (74*B*) and the knight's file would be open for the rook (76); also, a bishop is normally worth just a shade more than a knight. *B* shows the position if both of these captures were made.

109

Simply to pin a knight is not enough: the move must be part of a larger plan. A common idea is an advance in the centre which the pinned knight cannot prevent. *A* and *B* show this idea in its simplest form: in both positions White is free to advance the rear pawn to secure an aggressive pawn centre. Another possibility is piece play against the weak knight. *C* shows it under attack from a second man, a white knight. Now White can wreck Black's pawn position by capturing with either piece since Black would have to recapture with the pawn or lose his queen. A typical continuation for White after the exchange of knights would be an attack against the rook (*D*).

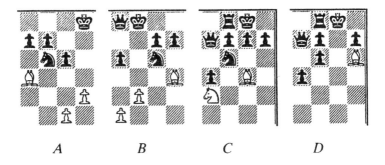

| *A* | *B* | *C* | *D* |

The main danger here is not to the rook (which can move away) but to the king who now stands open to attack.

As Black cannot at once escape the situation in *C*, White may do better to delay the capture of the knight. Do not be in a hurry to seize an opportunity that will still be available next move.

110 *Fighting the Pin*

Now consider the pin from the defender's viewpoint. A common idea is to attack the bishop at once with the rook's pawn (*A*), forcing it either to capture the knight or to try to keep the pin by moving back a square. This pawn move has the additional advantage of allowing the king an escape square against the possibility of a mating threat on the back rank later on.

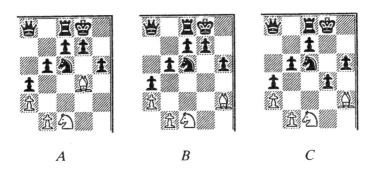

A   B   C

If the attacker retreats, let us consider this new position (*B*). At any time Black now has the option of moving up his knight's pawn two squares, attacking the bishop and at the same time freeing the knight from the pin (*C*). This second advance may or may not be good for, although forcing the bishop off the diagonal, it will likely weaken the pawn position. This could be a very dangerous manoeuvre on the same side as the castled king, as here.

The one-square move of the rook's pawn is frequently

played in the opening to stop an embarrassing pin; but the move should not be freely used as it is rather too peaceful – it is sometimes called the 'country move!' These same ideas are seen where the knight is pinned against the king, though here the attack may be less strong since the action will be on the queen's side and the king will probably castle on the other wing.

111

There are several ways in which a defender may free himself from a pin and yet prevent his pawn wall from being broken. Let us consider the case where the knight is pinned against the queen (A). Here White can unpin the knight by playing his queen up two squares (B). As the queen still defends the knight, Black cannot double the white pawns by exchanging. In C, the pin is released by a bishop move. Another defence is to play the second knight to guard his companion (D): this does not free the pin at once but does permit the queen to move where she pleases without allowing the pawns to be broken.

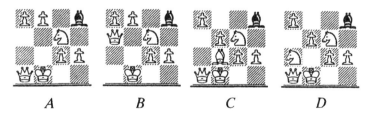

| A | B | C | D |

112

Where the knight is pinned against the king we have these same ideas to prevent the break-up of the pawns. The king can then be moved to safety, ideally by castling. If there is a risk that the exchange of bishop for knight will weaken the pawn position, it is important to castle on the opposite side of the board otherwise the king may be open to attack.

113

Knights developed on the second rank only attack one central square and often interfere with the free movement of the other pieces. However, there are several situations where such a move may be necessary. A knight may be played to one of these squares to avoid a pin (an attacking bishop can be driven off by advancing the c- or f-pawn) or in passage to another square or to defend a weakness as in 111*D* above.

114

It is time now to look at a few openings. In a book of this size it is hopeless even to attempt a general picture of the possibilities. The few examples that follow have therefore been chosen not because they are commonly met with (they are not) but because they illustrate some typical opening ideas.

Do not try to follow these openings move by move in your games but use them rather as models from which to develop plans of your own.

115

OPENING 1 – *Giuoco Piano*

	White	Black
1.	e4	e5
2.	Nf3	Nc6
3.	Bc4	Bc5

This opening has already been mentioned (102). 'Knights out first, and then bishops' is an old saying and good advice.

4. c3

Preparing the advance of the d-pawn. White strives for a strong pawn centre.

4. . . .   Nf6

Black counters by attacking the undefended e-pawn.

5. d4   exd4
6. cxd4   Bb4 ch

Black had no time to take the e-pawn because his bishop was attacked.

7. Bd2

Black could now play 7. . . . Nxe4; and there might follow 8. Bxb4, Nxb4; 9. Bxf7 ch (a temporary sacrifice that regains the pawn), Kxf7; 10. Qb3 ch, followed by Qxb4 and an equal game.

7. . . .   Bxd2 ch

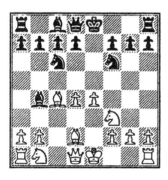

Position after White's 7th
move

Position after Black's 11th
move

8. Nbxd2

Now White guards the e-pawn whilst developing a piece.

8. ...   d5

It was essential for Black to counter White's strong centre. White will now be left with an isolated d-pawn, a situation common to several openings (in the game in Part Five, White got an isolated d-pawn in quite a different way). The positional weakness of this pawn is balanced by its influence on the centre.

9. exd5   Nxd5
10. Qb3   Nce7

Defending the king's knight which is twice attacked. Black could not move the threatened piece because he would lose a pawn (to 11. Bxf7 ch) when also his king would be unable to castle. A king who cannot castle in the opening is in a dangerous position. Notice the White queen has come out to a square where she exerts pressure but cannot well be attacked.

11. 0–0   0–0

Both sides move their king to safety (see diagram). White will now play his rooks to files where their powers can be better used – probably to the c- and e-files. Black has still to develop his bishop but has an about equal game, thanks to his strong knight on d5.

116

OPENING 2 – *Four Knights' Game*

	White	*Black*
1.	e4	e5
2.	Nf3	Nc6
3.	Nc3	Nf6
4.	Bb5	Bb4
5.	0–0	0–0
6.	d3	Bxc3

So far a model of rapid development. Black exchanged bishop for knight here because the knight was likely to prove a better piece than the bishop. For example, White might later have played Bg5 followed by Nd5 (the same idea as in 109*C*) when the black bishop's only use would have been in defence.

7.	bxc3	d6
8.	Bg5	Qe7

Black's last move is not easy to understand. It does three things: it prepares to unite the rooks after a bishop move, it gives additional protection to the e-pawn which may be needed if White plays d4 (black would not wish to exchange this pawn as this would undouble the white pawns and also give ground in the centre) and lastly it prepares Black's next move which is part of his plan. Check from the diagram that you have the position right.

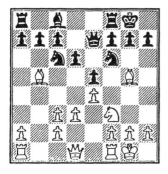

Position after Black's 8th
move

Position after White's 13th
move

| 9. | Re1 | Nd8 |
| 10. | d4 | Ne6 |

Another way to attack a pinning bishop.

11. Bc1

Sometimes a bishop returns home and then comes out on the other diagonal. White has the better of the opening with more space in the centre and some attacking chances. Black's e-pawn is weak and to exchange it for White's d-pawn would only strengthen the white centre. If Black now developed the bishop with 11. . . . Bd7; and White played 12. Bc4 (if 12. Bxd7, Nxd7!), then 12. . . . Bc6? (With the idea of meeting 13. dxe5 with Nxe4) would be a terrible mistake on account of 13. d5! (remember the pawn fork (40D)? This might-have-happened disaster earns a diagram (above, right).

117

OPENING 3 – *Sicilian Defence*

	White	Black
1.	e4	c5

This is currently one of the most popular defences to the king's pawn opening (chess openings go in and out of fashion like other things). Black's move unbalances the central pawn position and is the signal for a hard fight.

2.	Nf3	d6
3.	d4	cxd4
4.	Nxd4	Nf6
5.	Nc3	a6

This move was played to prevent the square b5 being used by one of the white minor pieces, and to prepare an advance of the b-pawn which would allow the QB to be developed at b7. We saw this same idea in the game in Part Five. Black also plans an attack on the queen's side, so this moves combines both attack and defence.

6.	Bg5	e6

Black permits the pin. For one reason, he must get his KB out.

7.	f4	Be7
8.	Qf3	Qc7

This move stops both the advance of the e-pawn and the development of white's bishop at the good square c4. Check your position against the diagram.

Position after Black's
8th move

Position after Black's
10th move

9. 0–0–0

Our first example of queen's-side castling. The rook is at once activated and White will now be free to advance the king's-side pawns to attack the black king's position. Black will probably have to castle on the king's side as he has weakened the pawn position on the queen's side.

9.	...	Nbd7
10.	Bd3	b5

The position offers many tactical possibilities and the chances are about even. White now has the double attack 11. e5, threatening the knight and at the same time uncovering a queen attack on the rook. However, Black too has tactical play and all sorts of violence could follow. This is a typical Sicilian scrap, wild and complicated.

118

OPENING 4 – *Queen's Gambit*

White	*Black*
1. d4	d5
2. c4	

This move gives the opening its name. A GAMBIT is the sacrifice of a man in the opening with the idea of gaining space or time or both. Often the man given up (usually a pawn) is recovered later. A good way to deal with gambits is to accept the sacrifice and return the offer at a suitable moment.

> **2. . . .   e6**

But here the gambit is refused – *declined* we say. Black plans to set up a solid if rather cramped position. The second player is at a small disadvantage in the opening (he is, after all, a move behind) and must avoid delay.

> **3. Nc3   Nf6**
> **4. Bg5**

If Black now accepts the gambit with 4. . . . dxc4; White could advance strongly in the centre with 5. e4, at the same time attacking the black pawn with his KB.

> **4. . . .   Be7**

The pin is awkward, so Black frees himself by one of the methods we saw in (111). 4. . . . Nbd7; is also often played here, setting a well-known trap: 5. cxd5, exd5; 6. Nxd5?, Nxd5! (surprise!); 7. Bxd8, Bb4 ch. Now White has only one move: 8. Qd2, and after 8. . . . Bxd2 ch; 9. Kxd2, Kxd8; Black is a piece ahead. There are several such traps in the openings. Never allow yourself to feel that your or your opponent's position is impregnable!

Black would have been wrong to try 4. . . . h6; instead of 4. . . . Be7; for White could then have continued 5. Bxf6. Now if Black recaptures with the queen (5. . . .

Qxf6) he loses a pawn after 6. cxd5, exd5; 7. Nxd5, or if he recaptures with the pawn (5. . . . gxf6) his position on the king's side is wrecked with 6. cxd5, exd5. Play through these variations and you will see that in the first White gets a material advantage and in the second a positional advantage, showing how important it is to handle pins correctly.

5.	**e3**	**0–0**
6.	**Nf3**	**Nbd7**
7.	**Bd3**	**dxc4**

**Position after Black's
4th move**

**Position after Black's
10th move**

Black forces the bishop to move again before striking in the centre.

8.	**Bxc4**	**c5**
9.	**0–0**	**a6**
10.	**a4**	**b6**

Black with his 9th move was trying for a rapid advance

119

on the queen's side, gaining space and forcing the white bishop to move once again. White's 10th move countered this idea. Look back to the comment after Black's 10th move in the game in Part Five. With his 10th move here, Black prepares to develop his QB at b7 – the easiest way. Both sides have nearly completed development. Before the battle proper begins each player will probably seek a safe square for his queen to allow the rooks freedom on the back rank. The game is fairly level.

119

OPENING 5 – *King's Indian Defence*

	White	Black
1.	Nf3	Nf6
2.	c4	g6
3.	g3	Bg7

In this defence, Black attacks the centre from a distance, delaying a pawn advance until White commits himself.

4.	Bg2	

The development of a bishop in this way is known as a fianchetto. Both sides have fianchettoed their king's bishops which attack the centre from safe positions.

	White	Black
4.	. . .	d6
5.	d4	0–0
6.	0–0	c6

Fianchettoed bishops add security to castled kings (73C).

7. Nc3   a6

This strange-looking move is to prepare a general advance on the queen's side starting with b5. Positions like this (see diagram) are commonly seen today whereas they were unknown a few years ago – proof both of the development of the game and of changing fashions. Black does not at once contest the centre but is hopeful that White will present targets there for him to strike at later; but he cannot leave it too late or White will take control and the Black position will become very tight. Another feature of this type of opening is that opportunities arise for *transposition* – that is, for a known position in another opening to be reached by a different order of moves. For example, it is possible for a King's Indian Defence to transpose into well-known variations of the Sicilian Defence (Opening 3). However, these are refinements you need not trouble about at present, but you should avoid playing this kind of 'clever' opening as Black unless you have a clear plan which must of course include a challenge in the centre.

8.	e4	Bg4
9.	h3	Bxf3
10.	Qxf3	e5

Black exchanges his bishop because it has little freedom and the white knight is strong in the centre. When Black played 8. . . . Bg4 he had to be prepared to exchange if the bishop was attacked as he cannot retreat to h5 (maintaining the pin) on account of White playing g4, winning a piece for two pawns as the bishop has no retreat. True, this would have resulted in the opening of White's king's position, but the black pieces are not well placed for attack

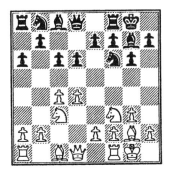

Position after Black's
7th move

Position after Black's
12th move

and White would keep a clear material advantage.

There was another tactical possibility in the position. If White had played 9. e5 (instead of 9. h3) he would have lost a pawn after 9. . . . dxe5; 10. dxe5. Now the second white pawn is alone and too far advanced to be defended. After 10. . . . Nfd7, the pawn is attacked twice. If White now gave up the pawn by 11. e6, Black would capture it with the bishop. 11. . . . fxe6 would be bad as it would leave Black with doubled and isolated pawns in the centre.

11.	Be3	Nbd7
12.	Rfd1	Qe7

White has a slight advantage in this position (see diagram). You might here be thinking about the value of the different minor pieces in relation to the pawn structure. It is quite possible, for example, that White's KB may prove 'bad' in the ending – and so might Black's. White's QB, on the other hand, looks as though it will be useful and should not be exchanged.

120

The openings you have played through have been worked out and used by masters. Each example given is only one, shortened line within a large family of lines in that particular opening. These are all set out in the reference books, but I urge you not to start learning openings by heart. It is much better that you 'free-think' your way through the openings for a while. Experience will quickly bring shape to your ideas and you will then be better prepared to improve your game with further study if you so wish.

And don't forget that it takes two players to make an opening: for a start, your opponent may not help you by doing what you expect him to do. If it seems he has made a weak move, consider what you would have done in his place and then see if any advantage can be taken of the fact that he has not played it. Do try to see what he is plotting: it is easy to be so enchanted with one's own plans that one overlooks what the other side is doing! Finally, if your opponent plays wildly do not be tempted into wild play yourself – it can be catching and it does not make for good chess.

PART SEVEN

The End Game

121

You may wonder why we have passed from the Opening to the End Game, leaving out the Middle Game.

The middle game is the battle proper in which you have to find your own way helped by a few guiding principles and your own experience. We have already studied these principles in the Parts on Tactics and, particularly, Strategy. The opening and the end game, on the other hand, lend themselves to study. If you start the game well, you will enter the middle game with confidence and if you understand the end game you will be confident of where you are going in the middle game.

122

The end game may be described as that stage of the game in which both sides are so reduced in forces as to be unable to win by direct attack. A typical end game might have on the board, apart from the kings, one or two pieces and a number of pawns on each side. Although the end game comes at the end of a game, not all games have an end game: some finish in the middle game or even, as we saw in Part Six, in the opening. Also, end games can be very long – sometimes longer than the opening and middle game together.

123

There are other features of the end game. Because the forces are reduced, so is the danger to the kings who can now become active, fighting pieces. For the same reason, the value of the remaining pawns is greatly increased as prospects for promotion are much brighter. Both sides, too, have more space to move about in, which often means that there is a wider choice of plans than there is in the middle game. This does not mean a wider choice of good plans; usually there is only one good plan in an ending.

The skills you need to know for the end game can be reduced to two:

(*a*) Promoting a pawn.
(*b*) Mating with a small force.

124

Of course, the end game is not as easy as that, in fact it is probably the most difficult part of chess, but these are the two skills that will be in most demand.

In the end game, because of the few men engaged, the same kinds of positions recur many times. It is for this reason that the end game, like the opening but unlike the middle game, has been deeply studied. The correct way to handle different types of ending have been developed over many years, even centuries, so that today much hard thinking is saved for us; which does not mean that memory is enough, for in the end game, as in all chess, understanding is the first essential. It is not even enough to play the right moves: they must also be played in the right order.

125
King and Pawn v. *King*

The ending of king and pawn against king is not only a common one, it is a basic one. Any game in which one side is a pawn ahead can, in theory, be reduced by exchanges to this three-man battle. With a bigger material advantage of course, the stronger side should find his problems easier.

The elements of this ending are not difficult. No checkmate is possible with king and pawn against king: set the three men on the board and try and construct a mating position with them and you will see that it cannot be done. For the stronger side to win it is therefore necessary to promote the pawn.

The defence by the solitary king is first to try to capture the pawn. If the other king cannot interfere, there is a simple way to decide whether or not a pawn can be caught.

Look at *A* and imagine a 'magic square', one side being the distance from the square on which the pawn stands to its queening square, the other of course the same distance along the rank. As the pawn advances, this 'magic square' is reduced in size. The rule is that the opposing king can

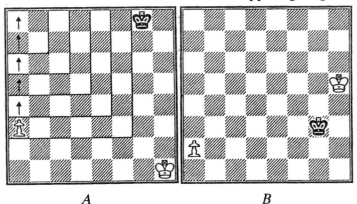

A　　　　　　　　　B

126

catch the pawn if he is within the 'magic square' or can enter it.

If the pawn is on its starting square (*B*), do not forget to allow for the initial double move. In both examples, Black, with the move, can catch the pawn, but if White moves first the pawn will safely queen.

126

If the pawn can be defended, then the lone king should try to place himself in its path. Unless he now gives way the pawn is unable to queen and the game is therefore drawn. However, there are several positions where the lone king can be forced aside by the opposing king. This 'battle of the kings' is an important part of king and pawn endings, though really it is more like a ballet than a battle as the kings cannot, as we know, attack each other. Frequently, however, they approach each other; if the two kings stand face to face with one square between them, the king that moves first has to give way. Neither king can advance in diagram *A*. Let us suppose that the black king must move (*B*), then the white king can go forward one rank (*C*). Now the black king can also move down one rank (*D*) but again the white king can go forward (*E*) and you will see

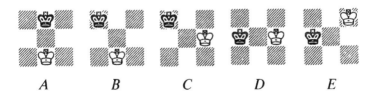

A	*B*	*C*	*D*	*E*

that White is a move ahead. This extra move is often vital in the end game where the first player to promote a pawn usually wins. Any other move for the black king in *A* would be at least as bad as that played.

127

Why are king moves so important? Look at *A*. White's pawn is two steps from becoming a queen and the kings are facing each other: there are no other pieces on the board. If White moves first, he can only draw, but if Black is to play, White wins. Follow the play carefully for this small battle will occur many times in your end games.

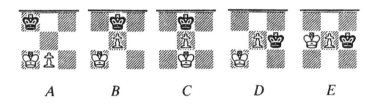

| A | B | C | D | E |

If White advances the pawn, giving check, the black king will move in front of it (*B*). What is White to do? He cannot move the pawn again, and if he moves the king to keep guard on it, the black king is stalemated (*C*). Any other move of the white king will allow Black to capture the pawn.

Alternatively, White can, in *A*, move his king to any of four squares (these are not included in the mini-board but may be easily imagined), but the black king can then move in front of the pawn and White can make no progress.

The game is a draw as White cannot promote the pawn.

If Black moves first he must place his king in front of the pawn. White now advances the pawn and the position in *B* is again reached but this time with Black to play. There is only one move (*D*), when White can play up his king (*E*) and the pawn will be safely queened next move. The mate of king and queen against king is then easily forced, as we shall see.

128

The Opposition

This is a striking example of what is called the OPPOSITION – a situation where the two kings face each other. The side who is forced to move his king is said *not* to have the opposition. Notice that the positions of the kings in *A* and *E* correspond to their positions in 126 *A* and *D*.

It is possible to have also a *diagonal opposition* (the kings on the same diagonal with one square between them) and a *distant opposition*, when the kings are farther apart. It is often a winning advantage to have the opposition in king and pawn end games. If there are pieces on the board as well, however, the opposition may be of little or no importance.

129

Let us now inspect other possible endings of king and pawn against king where the pawn is supported and the defender can get his king ahead of the pawn on the same file. *In the case of a rook's pawn the game is a draw whoever has the move.* Look at *A*. Here we have 127*A* again but at the edge of the board. If Black is to move, he goes into the corner and the pawn advances (*B*) – White can make no headway with king moves. Now we have position 127*B* again except, because the black king is on the rook's file, he cannot be forced to move out on the other side of the pawn. The position is stalemate.

A   B   C   D   E

Even if a defender cannot reach the rook's file, the ending is still often drawn. Look at *C*. The game is drawn whoever moves first. If White moves, he must play up his king and Black moves to keep the opposition (*D*) although he could also draw here by attacking the pawn. Now if White advances the pawn it is his turn to be stalemated. If Black moves first, White does no better. If he moves his king back to free his pawn (*E*) the black king goes to the knight's file and we have the draw shown in *A*.

130

In cases where the pawn is not a rook's pawn and the defending king can reach the queening square of the pawn, the attacker will win if his king is two or more squares ahead of his pawn because he can always use a pawn move to get the opposition. Where the attacker's king is one square in front or level with his pawn, he may win if he has the opposition.

131

With several pawns on the board in addition to the kings, the player who has more usually wins. The aim of the stronger side in these cases is to force a passed pawn or to exchange pawns until a won K & P *v*. K ending is reached.

Where both sides have the same number of pawns, the player whose king is better placed can sometimes win. These remarks refer to positions in which the pawn formations are *uncompromised*; that is, those that do not include doubled or backward pawns. See diagram *A*. Here White has an uncompromised pawn majority on the king's side and so can force a passed pawn by playing up his rook's pawn two squares. Whether or not Black now exchanges pawns, the black king will be outside the 'magic square'. If Black plays first in *A*, however, he advances his pawn and the white pawn majority is compromised since the rook's pawn is backward (*B*). In fact, White would now lose quickly for since his king cannot move, he must play up his rook's pawn. Whether it is moved one square or two, Black will capture it (don't forget 'en passant' – 24). Now the second white pawn can move so there is no

A   B

stalemate. The black pawn promotes to queen at the same time giving checkmate.

If, in position *A*, the men on the left-hand side had all been one square over to the right, White, with the move, could only have drawn as the black king would have been able to move inside the 'magic square'. This would have allowed the white king to capture the black pawn next to him and both sides would have been left with bare kings.

132

It is quite common with equal pawns to find majorities on opposite wings. Thus in 131 above White has a pawn extra on the king's side, Black on the queen's side. It is also common in endings to find the kings near to each other. Where these situations occur (pawns unbalanced, kings together), again as in 131, it is favourable to have the pawn majority on the side away from the kings – and the farther away the better. This is true whether or not there are pieces on the board and it is one of those points you should bear in mind when exchanging men in the late middle game.

133 *Stopping Pawn Promotion*

The first defensive duty of a piece in the end game (apart from preventing checkmate) is to stop enemy pawns promoting. The action necessary against a passed pawn takes one of three forms. These are, in preferred order:

(*a*) Capture the pawn;
(*b*) Stop the pawn advancing by attacking a square in its path (as in 72*F*);
(*c*) Sacrifice the piece for the pawn if it will otherwise queen.

It is not, of course, possible to sacrifice the king to stop a pawn promoting and it would be pointless to give up the queen for this purpose, but these are the only exceptions.

134

A single, unsupported pawn whose path is clear is easily captured by king, queen or rook, but it can always escape capture by a bishop or a knight by moving ahead when it is attacked. A minor piece should therefore be moved not to attack the pawn but to attack a square in front of it. If this is not entirely clear to you it would be wise to work it out on a board.

135

If one pawn is easily stopped, two pawns together need care. If the pawns are far from promotion the task of the pieces it not hard. In *A*, *B* and *C* the pawns are held whichever side moves. If White has no move elsewhere on the board, then both pawns are lost in each case. Play these through: you will find that the advanced pawn must be attacked in *C*.

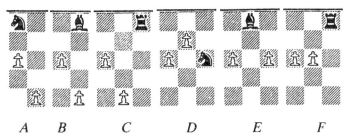

A   B   C   D   E   F

If the pawns are farther advanced, it may not be possible to stop one of them queening. In the next three examples (*D*, *E* and *F*) the pieces are helpless whichever side moves first. White gives up a pawn to promote the other in each case. Again, you would do well to work these out.

136

The queen deals easily with several pawns and the king too can stop a pair of passed pawns even if they are far advanced. *A* shows such a situation. The pawns cannot get through however White plays – the king even has a choice of squares. *B*, *C* and *D* are three possible continuations. The king is always free to move and keep guard on the

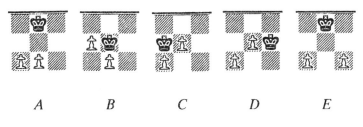

A   B   C   D   E

pawns but he can never take the rear pawn without allowing the other to queen. This is a common grouping which may occur anywhere on the board: the pawns are safe from attack by the king but cannot force their way past. If the white king arrives to help however a pawn will have easy passage to queen.

It is curious that sometimes two isolated pawns can present a greater threat than two united pawns which are otherwise much stronger. In *E*, the king is unable to move without allowing one of the pawns to promote.

If White is forced to move in any of the positions *B–E*, both pawns will be lost in every case.

It is a good general rule that passed pawns should not be allowed to advance further than necessary: the nearer a pawn is to queen, the greater is the danger for the defence.

137
Minor Piece Endings

In the ending king and minor piece against king and one or more pawns, the player with the piece cannot win. He should try and capture the pawn(s), giving up the piece if necessary, in order to draw.

138

In the ending king, minor piece and pawn against bare king the stronger side always wins with one important exception. *A rook's pawn and a bishop not of the same colour as the queening square of the pawn can only draw where the defending king can reach the queening square.* This ending is more common than you might imagine. In *A* you will see that whoever moves White can neither mate nor force the pawn through.

Where both sides have a minor piece and pawns, the side with the most pawns should usually win but again there is an exception and again this involves the bishop on account of its one-colour move. *If both sides have one bishop, and they are on opposite-coloured squares, then even an advantage of two pawns may not be enough to win.* B and C illustrate this: the weaker side takes control of the squares of one colour and the stronger side can do nothing to improve his position.

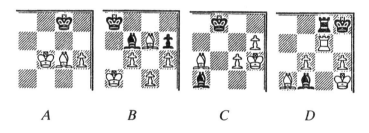

A   B   C   D

The *bishops of opposite colour* (as these are called) have an important part in the game. As the end game approaches, or even earlier, the weaker side may play to obtain them in the hope of eventually reaching a position similar to *B* or *C*. This is an idea which can be missed in the general battle. Look at *D*. Black is badly placed for he is two pawns behind; however, the right bishops are there and he has only to exchange the rooks to draw.

If other pieces are on the board as well as the bishops, and these pieces cannot be easily exchanged, then the opposite-colour bishops may be of no help to the weaker side.

139

Where each side has only a bishop left, apart from pawns, but the bishops are on the same coloured squares, then the better-placed side will sometimes win even if the forces are level.

140

A great deal could be written about the bishop *v.* knight duel in the end game. In general, a knight is best in a close position and where it can attack weak squares of both colours (though not of course at the same time). A bishop is better where there are pawns on both sides of the board. Sometimes a bishop can contain (that is, limit the movement of) a knight, as in *A*, and sometimes it is the knight who can contain the bishop (*B*). When a minor piece can be trapped, like the knight in *A*, it is often possible simply to walk up the king and take it.

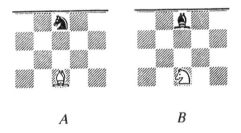

A	*B*

141

An advantage that the bishop has over the knight is that it can usually 'lose' a move, which the knight cannot. In *A*, White plays up the bishop one square, stopping the black pawn from moving and keeping guard on the queening square of the white pawn. Now the knight must move and the pawn will queen.

There is an important idea in this ending also – the 'good' and 'bad' bishop (77). The bishop is 'good' in *B* for it is on the same-coloured squares as the enemy pawns. A sacrifice quickly decides the game: 1. Bxg6 ch! and White will queen a pawn however Black plays. An example of a 'bad' bishop is shown in *C*. White wins by bringing the

136

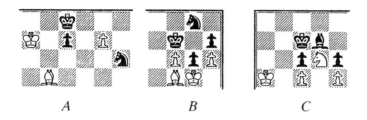

A   B   C

king up (always a sound idea in the end game if there is no obvious play). 1. Ka6. Now if Black checks, White reaches a won pawn ending: 1. . . . Bc8 ch; 2. Nxc8, Kxc8; 3. Kb6, Kd7; 4. Kb7 (the opposition!). The pawn is now lost and White will force a queen. Note these king moves: this is a common winning strategy where one king is well advanced. If the black king moves away he fares no better: 1. . . . Kd8; 2. Kb7, Ke7; 3. Kc7 and Black, with nothing attacked, is in zugzwang (31).

Like the 'opposite colour' bishops, the 'good' and 'bad' bishop are something to think about before the end game is reached.

142
Rook and Pawn Endings

Rook and pawn end games are the most common and often the most difficult. To play them well can take long study but we shall be content to keep our aims few and simple and to avoid the bad mistakes.

The first point to bear in mind is that king and rook alone can force mate against a bare king. Where one side has a rook and the other side a pawn only guarded by the king, the stronger side will always win if he can bring his king next to the pawn which can then be captured by the rook.

If the stronger side cannot do this, then the game is drawn because the rook will have to be given up for the

pawn when it promotes to queen as the ending K & Q v.
K & R is, with correct play, lost for the weaker side.

In *A*, White draws by advancing the pawn, but he must
be careful in responding to rook checks. After 1. b6, Rc4
ch; 2. Kd8 (or d7 or d6), and if the rook checks again, the
king must move back to the c-file. If the king moves too
far from the pawn the rook will capture it, and if he moves
in front of the pawn (for example, with 2. Kb7) Black will

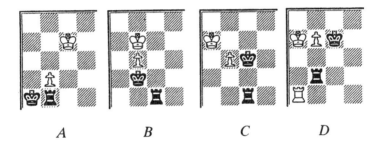

A　　　　*B*　　　　*C*　　　　*D*

have time to bring his king back, and the pawn will fall.

Study this second case as an example of the care that
must be taken in a 'simple' ending like this one. After 1.
b6, Rc4 ch; 2. Kb7?, Kb5; the position in B is reached.
White plays 3. Ka7, preparing to advance the pawn.
Black's best reply is Kc6 as this forces mate sooner,
though he could also play 3. . . . Ra4 ch; 5. Kb7, Ra6 and
the pawn is lost next move.

After 3. . . . Kc6; White has only a choice of losing
moves. Let us *analyse* the ending from here on (that is,
consider every possibility), not because it is an important
ending but simply as an exercise in 'chess thinking'. From
position C then, we will examine each line of play based
on White's move at this point.

138

(*a*) 1. Ka6, Ra4 mate

(*b*) 1. Kb8, Kxb6;
    2. Ka8, Rc8 mate

(*c*) 1. Ka8, Kxb6;
    2. Kb8, Rc5;
    3. Ka8, Rc8 mate

(*d*) 1. b7, Ra4 ch;
    2. Kb8, Rb4;
    3. Ka8, Kc7;
    (note 3. . . . Rxb7? stalemate!)
    4. b8(Q) ch, Rxb8 ch;
    5. Ka7, Rb6;
    6. Ka8, Ra6 mate

or

    3. Kc8, Rxb7;
    4. Kd8, Kd6;
    5. Ke8, Ra7;
    6. Kf8, Ke6;
    7. Kg8, Kf6;
    8. Kh8, Kg6;
    9. Kg8, Ra8 mate

The basic case in rook and pawn endings is rook and one pawn against rook. The rule here is that if the defending king can move in front of the pawn the game is almost always drawn (similar, you will notice, to a K & P *v.* K ending). The winning method for the stronger side is to get his king guarding the promotion square and sheltered from checks by using his own rook as an umbrella (*D* above). In this example, White can win in two ways, by checking with the rook to drive the king away and then promoting the pawn, or by promoting the pawn at once, allowing the black rook to take the new-born queen, and then checking the king so that it is driven away from the defence of the rook which will be captured by the white king.

143

A simple rule to remember in these endings is *rooks*

behind passed pawns. This is true whether you are trying to promote your pawn or stop your opponent's pawn; it is also good advice for the middle game too!

In *A*, the black rook is behind the passed pawn and is therefore better placed than the white rook. You can see, for example, that the black rook can move up and down the rook's file and still keep watch on the advanced white pawn but the white rook is unable to move without leaving the pawn 'en prise'.

This is a drawn ending. If the white king moves up to defend the pawn in order to free the rook to allow the pawn to promote, the black rook can check him away and then return to the rook's file to keep the attack on the pawn.

Now consider *B*. Here we have the same position but with the rooks reversed with the white rook behind the pawn and the black rook in front of it. White wins easily

A   B

by moving up his king when Black will have to give up his rook for the pawn or allow it to queen.

144

In rook and pawn endings where there is more than one pawn on the board and in many other endings we have not space to look at here, there are two ideas to keep in mind:

(*a*) The side that is ahead in material should normally win;

(*b*) The winning method for the stronger side is to reduce the position to one of the basic endings we have been looking at.

The stronger side can usually force the play as the weaker side is likely to have less choice of moves. An exchange or even a sacrifice may then be made at the right time.

145 *Queen and Pawn Endings*

In the king and queen *v.* king and pawn ending the stronger side has only to place his queen in front of the pawn and then to bring up his king to capture it. You will find that there is no way for the weaker side to force the queen aside as *the queen is the one piece that can never be approached by a king.*

The only position that gives a little difficulty is that where the pawn is already on the seventh rank and the promotion square is attacked by the king so that the queen cannot occupy it (*A*). White still wins from any position by reaching the situation shown in *B*. This he can easily do by a series of checks as the black king must guard the pawn and also stop the queen occupying the promotion square. Now the king must go in front of the pawn when the white king can be brought nearer. Black would then move his king away again threatening to promote and White would continue as before, forcing position B again. When the white king arrives next to the pawn checkmate will quickly follow.

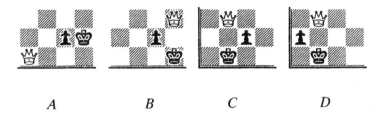

A   B   C   D

If the pawn on the seventh rank happens to be a bishop's or rook's pawn however, the weaker side can draw by a stalemate threat. C is a similar situation to B except that the pawn is on a bishop's file. Black to move here can play his king in the corner threatening to promote, and if the pawn is taken he is stalemated. Similarly in D with a rook's pawn. Here the king again goes into the corner and the queen must move away to avoid the stalemate. As in both C and D White will find no time to bring his king up, he must give the draw.

146
We have seen how to promote pawns in order to get the big material advantage to force checkmate against any defence, and also how to stop pawns queening. This is one of the two skills that are most needed in the end game. The second skill (look back to 123) is how to checkmate with a small force when all the pawns have gone from the board.

A single pawn, if it can be promoted, is enough to win. However, a single knight or bishop, worth three pawns in our table of values, is not.

Try to set up a checkmate position using king and knight or bishop against king. You will discover that even with the lone king in the corner this cannot be done. With a king and rook against king, however, mate is not only possible but can always be forced. This is the minimum mating force and is a common ending among students. It would be a common ending among experts too if it were not so well known that the weaker side will always resign the game at this point (if not before), being without hope. King and rook against king can be said to be the most important of all chess endings – if you cannot mate when the enemy king is defenceless you will not win many games!

147

The method of winning is straightforward but needs some attention. *The plan, which is common to all piece endings, is to drive the king to the edge of the board and to checkmate him there.* This checkmate we saw in 58*B* and in 61*B*. You may like to refresh your memory by looking back at these examples before going on.

Now follow through the sequence of play which is the same wherever the rook and kings are on the board.

(*a*) The rook is played to a rank or file to act as a wall to prevent the lone king escaping towards the centre of the board. This rank or file will normally be the one next to that on which the enemy king stands.

(*b*) The other king is then brought up until the two kings face each other *with the stronger side to play* (see *A*). A check by the rook (*B*) will then force the king back a rank and this sequence is repeated until the black king is at the edge of the board where he is mated.

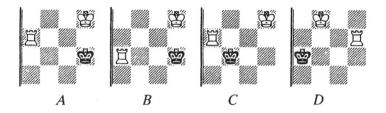

A   B   C   D

(c) The defender has two ways of delaying (but not avoiding) the mate. Firstly, by attacking the rook (C), when the correct play for White is to move the piece to the other side of the board *but staying on the same rank or file*. Secondly, by reaching a position similar to A with his (the defender's) turn to play. The right way to meet this manoeuvre may be to make a 'waiting' move with the rook, or to follow the lone king along with your king a knight's move away so that, when the edge of the board is reached (D), the enemy king will have to return opposite your king *when you have the move* (that is, position A again). A good example of this play was given in the second part of continuation (d) in the analysis in 142.

In this ending, the defender will not move back towards the board edge unless he is forced to do so as this will simply make the attacker's job easier.

It would be well to practise this important ending until you have it 'move perfect' – but remember always to make the best moves for your opponent too!

148

There are two minor-piece endings in which mate can be forced: king, bishop and knight or king and two bishops against king. Both endings require that the bare king be driven into a corner of the board, and in the case of the

144

bishop and knight ending, the corner must be that of the same colour as the square on which the bishop stands. Both these endings are very rare.

149

The ending king and queen against king is frequently seen (at least, among beginners) and easy to play. It is common because it often comes about from the promotion of the last pawn and is easy to play because the queen, being more powerful than the rook, can force back the enemy king quicker.

150

When attempting checkmate with a small force there is one comforting thought – a mistake (unless it is a very bad one) will not alter the result: the game will just go on a few more moves than was absolutely necessary. However, if you make too many small mistakes you may allow your opponent to escape with a draw under the fifty-move rule (101), so do not check around idly just because you have a solitary king to play with!

151

In all these endings the danger of a stalemate exists (and many players continue with only a king in the hope of just that). It is rare in the rook ending and can only occur when the king is in the corner; *A* and *B* are examples. In the case of the queen ending, however, the chance of stalemate is high. *C, D* and *E* are examples of which *C* is the most common.

The risk is also high in the minor piece endings *but in all cases the hunted king must be on the edge of the board for stalemate to occur*, so do not worry about this possibility too early!

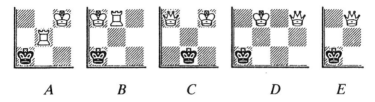

A   B   C   D   E

152

A weaker force than king and rook cannot give checkmate. We have already seen that a king and bishop or king and knight cannot mate even with the help of the lone king.

Although mate can occur in the ending king and two knights against king, *it cannot be forced* and this ending is properly a draw also.

A larger material advantage – for example, king, queen and bishop against king – should give you no difficulty whatever if you have mastered the basic endings given. Only one warning here: the stronger the force, the greater the risk of stalemate. It is not unknown for the student, umpteen pieces up, to stalemate the bare king in a planless effort to capture him!

153

The most important features of the end game have now been explained and your understanding of them will serve you well for some time yet. Later you may want to refer to one of the several good books available that list and describe every type of ending you are ever likely to meet.

PART EIGHT

The Next Steps

154

Learning to play chess is only the start of your pleasure –
and I hope that it has been a pleasure so far. Already you
have probably played a few games, your interest has
increased and you want to know what other opportunities
for play are open to you and what to do next to improve
your standard.

Perhaps most chessplayers get all they want out of the
game just by playing with friends. After all, life is a full
place and one cannot be an expert in everything.
However, only a little effort is needed to lift you above
this huge group of casual players and there is a lot to be
gained. If you are not already a member of a school or
other chess club you may wish to join one; it is likely there
is one locally. Soon you will have the opportunity for
match or tournament play which is more of a challenge
than friendly chess or 'skittles' as it is often called. In
competitive chess silence during play and 'touch and
move' are enforced, and you may also be expected to keep
a score of the game (score sheets are provided for
matches; you enter each move of both sides as it is played
and you are free to use any notation). One point is
awarded for a win and half a point for a draw, and the
winner is of course the side or player with the most points.

Later you may use a chess clock. This is two ordinary clocks in one unit, one clock recording the time you take for your moves and the other that taken by your opponent for his moves. Only the clock of the player whose turn it is to move is running at any one time. Clocks make sure that neither player sits and thinks (or perhaps just sits!) for too long. A typical rate of play is 24 moves in one hour which, as you are also free to think in your opponent's time, means an average of nearly five minutes for each move – slow enough!

Also, if you make your obvious moves quickly you have more time for those positions in which you need to think longer. A player who oversteps the time limit loses the game. Illustrated are a chess clock and (part of) a score sheet. Note the little 'flags' on the clock. The flag is lifted by the minute hand and drops on the hour to avoid dispute about the exact time taken.

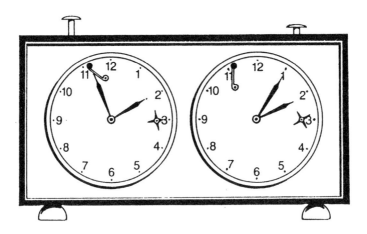

EVENT <u>CLUB CHAMPIONSHIP</u>
DATE <u>19th OCTOBER</u>   ROUND <u>4</u>

WHITE	A. Bishop		BLACK	A. Knight	
	WHITE	BLACK		WHITE	BLACK
1	N-f3	Nf6	25	gxh4	Nd3
2	c4	g6	26	a6	Nc5
3	g3	Bg7	27	axb7	Nxb7
4	Nc3	d6	28	dxc6	Resigns
5	d4	O-O	29		
6	Bg2	c6	30	1 — 0	
7	O-O	Nbd7	31		
8	e4	Rb8			
9	a4	Qc7			
10					

156

Unfinished Match Games

A match game unfinished when play is stopped is either *adjourned* or *adjudicated*.

(a) An *adjourned* game is one which is resumed at another time;

(b) An *adjudicated* game is one in which the players cannot agree a result and the position is passed to an expert for a verdict.

Certain procedures are called for in each of these cases. In an adjourned game, the player to move at close of play must write his move down without making the move on the board or telling his opponent what he has played. The move is put in an envelope which is then sealed. You are allowed to study an adjourned position if you wish (you would be silly if you did not!) and you may even seek advice on it although some players consider this unfair. The envelope is not opened until the game is restarted when the *sealed move*, as it is called, is made on the board. In an adjudicated game, the position at the close showing whose turn it is to move is passed by each player to his match captain with a claim as to the result.

157

If you are ambitious and wish to do more than play chess locally, there are events organized at regional and national level. Distance need not stop you either: correspondence chess (chess by post) is favoured by the handicapped and those living in out-of-the-way places, as well as those who like to analyse more deeply than an over-the-board game will allow.

158

More books have been written about chess, it has been said, than on all other games combined. This is at least doubtful, but certainly there is no lack of choice and eventually you may want to have a book on the openings and one on the endings, if only for reference. Later on, more specialized books or collections of master games may appeal to you.

159 *Chess Problems*

You will often find chess sections in newspapers and

magazines. A popular feature of these sections is a chess problem in which the reader is asked to checkmate in two or three moves. The only connection between the average chess problem and the game is that both follow the same rules of play.

A problem is a composition and a puzzle, and both position and play are usually unlike anything that would occur in a game. In a word, chess problems are something else; however, do not confuse problems with game positions which are also published in some papers and are becoming increasingly popular.

160

Now to improvement. Chess, as we said at the beginning, is a game of ideas and if you want to play it well you must develop your own plans, built upon and corrected by experience. Good ideas cannot be learnt. Question from the start the value of every move played. In a game, try to picture where a man would be well placed and see if you cannot get it there. Try to think in general terms but work out accurately every forced line of play. As in all games, you will profit from meeting players stronger than yourself.

Do not, however, accept without query what you are told. The worthwhile truth is the one that you prove to yourself.

Finally, a great deal can be got from playing through annotated games in books and magazines; but chess is for fun and one should not make it a labour. When all is said, the most interesting, and sometimes the best chess is played by those who go their own way.

INDEX

The number in italic type after each reference refers to the section number and the number in brackets to the page on which the section can be found

The number in italic type after each reference refers to the section number and the number in brackets to the page on which the section can be found

NOTES

NOTES

NOTES

NOTES

NOTES